Navigating the RIDE of Change

A Journey to Wellness and Healing

By

Maria Malayter, PhD

Printed in the United States of America

First Printing, 2016

ISBN-13: 978-0692681572

Published by the Do What You Love Foundation
Aurora, Illinois

www.dowhatulovefoundation.org

Dedications

This book is dedicated to all the people I met on my journey navigating the RIDE of change. Each person was a gift of God's immeasurable grace.

It is dedicated to any individual who has experienced brain trauma.

It is dedicated to any individual that is seeking answers and new paths to move through change.

Without God, this book would not be possible. May this book do the work He intends for the people who read it.

Contents

Acknowledgements

We don't do life alone, we do life together. The book, the story, and insights are all part of God's plan. There were many people who were all part of my healing puzzle.

First and foremost, this book would not be possible without God. Nor would this book be possible without the many people who have touched my life during the healing and recovery process, and those who influence me today.

My family: Anna, Dawn, Jeff, Jake, Mitch, Angeline, Kristen, and Sue for the unending encouragement and support. My brothers, Matt and Fred, for helping financially. My dear friend and brother in Christ, John—I am forever in gratitude for how God guided you to help me.

My friends: I am humbled by your friendship along this journey. Many thanks for the words of encouragement, emails, Facebook messages, and love. Thank you to the many Alpha Sigma Alpha sorority sisters and students that stayed connected to me on the journey.

My church families: I am certainly an ecumenical person with involvement in many churches and individual ministries. My continued strength in faith came from these groups then and now: Faith Lutheran Church, Our Savior Lutheran Church, Naperville Presbyterian, St. Margaret Mary, Holy Hill, Unity of Naperville, Unity of Oak Park, St. Thomas the Apostle, The Orchard, Gary United Methodist, and the many healing arts communities. I give thanks for the choirs at Faith and Our Savior, as well as the music director, pastor, and lay leaders who helped along the journey. I thank God for the prayer shawl ministry, connections team, worship arts, youth ministry, assisting ministers, communion assistants, ushers, lectors, deacons, and new life ministry.

My wellness and guidance team: Stacey, Dr. K., Jody, Dr. E., Vickie, Dr. Z., Peter, Denise, Dr. B., and Andre.

My community: I am grateful for the many community groups and activities I was involved in to help me move forward. I specifically want to thank Webster University at Great Lakes for the support on my journey.

My artist community: Naperville Art League, Capture My Chicago.com, Naperville (sub) urban art walk, St. Thomas Arts Ministry, The Orchard Arts Ministry, Burning Bush Gallery at Gary United Methodist, GuruShots.com, Fine Arts America, and First Fridays Aurora.

My book guidance team: The book would not be possible without your talents and gifts in the world of publishing. Special thanks to Nicole Grant, my editor; Patti Parish, my graphic artist; and Leo Zarko, a fellow author and great connector of local resources.

To the many people I will never know who prayed for me—thank you!

Introduction

Change is inevitable. The seasons change. Our lives change. As humans, we tend to like things to stay the same, but we know that it's impossible to avoid change. We have to figure out ways to navigate and RIDE through change. My journey certainly involved a lot of change, and I had to adapt and shift gears. To me, life is like riding a bicycle. We face adversity, change, and bumps on the road. But to stay balanced on a bicycle, we have to keep pedaling and moving forward.

Do you remember riding a bicycle when you were younger? What did you experience? Perhaps freedom and change? As our lives change, our bicycles change. Did you start riding with a tricycle or a big wheel? What sticks out the most in my memory is my first two-wheeler bike with a leopard print banana seat. It was stylish and fun and led me to much adventure. I loved that bicycle and all that it represented. I changed into my teen years with a bicycle sporting yellow mag tires, and then transitioned into a ten-speed bicycle. In my mid-twenties I purchased a purple Schwinn Moab mountain bicycle with front tire shocks. My life changed and my bicycles changed, too. What was your progression of bicycles?

Navigating change is also like riding a bicycle; we have to ensure we have the right equipment and learn how to use it. There are many types of bicycles we can choose—fat tire or electric bikes, even unicycles if that's your thing—and there are a variety of paths we can embark on when navigating change. At times, we may have to adjust our seats, we might get a flat tire, and we will have bumps on the road. No matter what, the terrain of our bike path—and our lives—will change and we will have to ride on.

I know a lot about riding through change and cycling. In 2012, I biked over 1650 miles, that's nearly the distance from Chicago to Phoenix. In 2013, I biked over 1037 miles, which is the equivalent of Chicago to Denver, but it felt like 1600 miles because it was uphill. Last year, in 2014, I biked about 1222 miles, which was like riding to Salt Lake City from Chicago. In 2015, I biked about 1196 miles while navigating change in a new professor role.

Adding up the miles over the years...I'm tired...just kidding! It has been an amazing journey.

Riding my bike is one of the ways I cope with change. I returned to biking in 2010 after losing my job and having to reinvent myself. My dear friend Jason constantly spoke about his peaceful and joyful bicycle rides on the Fox River Trails, so he inspired me to get my bike tuned up and hit the trails. After more than 5100 miles, I still appreciate him each day I get on my bike, as it helps me deal with life and adversity.

There's nothing better than the peace and freedom experienced from riding a bike—unless you meet with change and adversity. For the younger me, that was Sammy, the mean neighborhood dog. You know, the one that has a bite that matches his bark. One perfect sunny day, I was cruising down the street—just me and my leopard print banana seat bike. I was at peace, full of joy, and relishing the freedom. I was cruising along, carefree, and you know what's next—it was time to let go of the handle bars, one hand at a time. It was blissful independence. Suddenly, adversity arrived! Sammy broke out of his fenced yard, ran right for me, and started trying to bite my leg. Heck it was like shark week—and Sammy won! His teeth got ahold of my leg, and I went flying over the handle bars, ending up with a dog bite and multiple bruises. Yes, I got bit by change and I got lots of bruises! I picked myself up, dragged myself home with my injuries and bike, feeling a mix of shock and anger. But do you know what? The next day, I grabbed my bike and rode on. Each day we have the choice to face change and ride on.

The Medical Path

It was a crisp early spring day outside of Chicago. The sun was making its appearance here and there, fighting the fast-moving clouds for center stage. There was no snow falling, and I, like many of my fellow Chicagoans, was thankful for that. I was driving my Toyota Corolla home from my morning bible study, mentally preparing for the day ahead. I had a lot to do for work that day and I was prioritizing my task list in my head when—Boom! I was thrown forward from sudden impact. I was shaken, slightly dazed, and had no idea what happened. I looked up and realized my car had hit the SUV that decided not to take the right-hand turn at the light after all. I felt the shock all over, even though my body had not hit anything within the car. When the other driver and I pulled over into the nearest parking lot, I saw the SUV I had collided into was unscathed, but my car was crumpled up like an aluminum can. The police arrived and immediately checked to see if I needed medical attention. I declined. We exchanged insurance information and the police filled out the report. My car was towed to a body shop, but the SUV was able to drive away from the incident. It was March 3, 2010, and my life was forever changed.

I picked up a rental car, and I decided to call my primary care physician's office to go in and get checked out physically as a precautionary measure. I was already starting to get a major headache, but I wasn't certain as to why, given the fact that I did not hit my head or any other body part during the accident. I thought it could have been from the stress of the ordeal, or simply that I was feeling hungry by that time.

I arrived at the doctor's office and was checked out by his medical team. They did x-rays to check for broken bones. Unsurprisingly, they found nothing. I was not feeling great at the time, and had some sinus congestion. They treated me for a sinus infection with a round of antibiotics and steroids. The staff thought the headaches were all related to the sinus infection. I didn't question their conclusion because I needed a quick solution to continue with my busy work week. I had a big week ahead of me as I was hosting the very first National Positive Aging Conference. It was being presented through the Center for Positive Aging, which I had leadership over. I had a seemingly endless list of details and plans to complete, and I needed to finalize my speeches for the conference.

Our event was right before the national conference of the American Society on Aging being held in Chicago. I was not only a speaker for the Positive Aging Conference but also a co-presenter for a workshop at the American Society on Aging Conference. I had planned to stay in the city for a couple of nights to ensure the Positive Aging Conference went well and to have full engagement with the American Society on Aging Conference. These events were taking place in the first few days following the accident, and I felt very different. I continued to have major headaches, my mind was racing, and I could not sleep. I felt as though my life was placed on fast-forward. At first I thought these symptoms could easily be attributed to the stress and excitement of all that was going on with the conferences. However, I soon noticed that my words started to slip out of my mouth before I could stop them, and sometimes they were highly inappropriate. My speech became completely unfiltered. I was uninhibited and I felt as though I was somewhat drunk. At this point, I knew my behavior was completely abnormal.

The difficult part was that even though I was not feeling right, I still needed to present at both of the conferences. The first conference was hosted by the Center for Positive Aging, where I was the director. I was the main leader and knew I had to carry through the event. People were flying in from all over the country to attend, and I wanted to make a good impression for the center. I made it through the Positive Aging Conference without any major incident, although I seemed to be more forgetful than usual.

The second conference was for the American Society on Aging. I was co-presenting a session with my colleague Rob, and I did not want to let him down, as he was preparing for a promotion. He and I spent many hours drafting the presentation long before the conference.

When the time came, Rob and I started our

presentation, "Careers in Aging," at the American Society on Aging Conference in Chicago. Our lecture was going well until we came to the question and answer portion. Someone asked a question about difficult legislation that was slowing the process to advance careers in the field of aging. I quickly became agitated and a swear word almost slipped out as I answered the question. I am usually very calm and poised when I am presenting, and I wasn't even sure why I was so agitated. My co-presenter's concern grew. He was worried about my behavior and fearful that I might swear during the presentation.

I could not understand why I was falling to pieces and getting agitated so easily. I continued to attend the conference, despite the difficulties I was having. I was unable to sleep at night, and I still felt as though my life was moving at warp speed. Everything was moving so quickly, and I was overstimulated by all the hustle and bustle in the city. Soon, it was the last day of the conference and I was planning to attend a special business summit on baby boomers. I felt uneasy, I was shaking and could not concentrate. I packed my things and asked the concierge at the hotel to call a taxi to take me home immediately. It was over an hour ride home, and it felt longer still. I was relieved to finally arrive at home in the suburbs to relax in nature and have less stimulation from the city. I phoned my primary care doctor for an appointment right away. I also decided to take a few days off of work following the conferences to heal from the car accident and sinus infection.

During my time off, the headaches persisted and became so intense that my doctor recommended a few paths for solutions. The first path I went on was to see a neurologist to explore the headaches. I also worked with a chiropractor to try to increase the range of motion in my neck. When the headaches persisted, we then added a physical therapist to help with the movement in my neck, which was severely limited by tight muscles. We were building a team to seek answers and find solutions, and my life was becoming a series of medical appointments.

I returned to work to find my job-related behaviors changing. I was experiencing significant memory loss, scattered thinking, and excessive frustration. I was speaking my mind during meetings without considering the outcome. The outspoken change in my personality led me to receive a referral to the Employee Assistance

Program (EAP) for counseling. My boss required many sessions, and it was recommended I take advantage of the Family and Medical Leave Act (FMLA) and take time off work to find out what happened and to heal.

It was during my leave of absence from work that people were starting to notice my personality was changing. Normally a positive and upbeat person, I now was quick to anger. I overreacted easily and often. I was uninhibited and started taking risks. For instance, when I was shopping in the grocery store and saw a really great outfit on a person I would tell them how beautiful they looked. At restaurants, I overheard conversations at nearby tables and I interrupted to give my opinions on what was being said, rudely butting in to other people's conversations. Frequently, I would tell my whole life story to the uninterested cashier at the store.

One of the riskier situations I got involved with was taking on the advocacy and fund-raising campaign for a homeless man named Billy Bob. He was an ex-convict who appeared to be living on the corner of Adams Street and Michigan Ave in downtown Chicago. I bought him food. I panhandled with him, holding a cup while standing by his side. I rallied to get him a home. I sought resources for him. But the truth is, some people like to remain homeless and some people who panhandle are not homeless. I'm pretty sure Billy Bob was the latter. I say this because he phoned me from a landline phone that I tracked back to a residence on North Lake Shore Drive, one of the most expensive residential areas in the city of Chicago. I was helping raise funds for someone who may not have been homeless. Six years later he is still panhandling in the same spot. Obviously I was not thinking clearly or rationally.

Thoughts popped into my mind and then the words just slipped out of my mouth. This new behavior and expressivity of mine made me feel as if I was walking around drunk all the time, like I had little control. I was thankful to be seeing a therapist when all of this started to occur. Together, with the rest of my medical team, we were trying to find ways to help me heal from whatever was going on.

My entire team was confused in their attempts to construct a path to healing for me. My primary care physician, my therapist, my chiropractor, a neurologist, and a physical therapist were all working in tandem to try and help me. Knowing how to heal from this situation seemed impossible because we had no idea what was causing the headaches and behavioral changes. I did not hit my head during the car accident so we never went down the path thinking there was a head injury. Every person's journey is very different when healing from a traumatic brain injury, mine was made more difficult by the fact that we did not think that was the problem. This made searching for solutions very confusing and unclear.

At one point in the journey my physician, Dr. Chez, recommended I see another mental health professional. I was still acting very different compared to my normal personality. In the initial assessment with a psychologist, Ms. Gully, I felt very uncomfortable and anxious. I do not remember the specific reason Dr. Chez sent me there, perhaps it was for a mental capacity assessment. Anyhow, the psychologist did not know me and was meeting me for the first time, when I was not acting in accordance with my normal personality and I was completely stressed out. Stress was causing additional challenges in my complex situation of trying to find the right way to heal.

The aftermath of that appointment was the worst. I had to keep current with the insurance companies on the reporting of treatment following the accident. At one

point I was clarifying the payment for the session with
the insurance representative on the phone. The insurance representative questioned the outcome and diagnosis in the session. Ms. Gully had prescribed several
major psychotropic medications and documented a
diagnosis of bipolar disorder. I was outraged and confused that my outgoing personality created a diagnosis
of this type. I could not understand how the major
stressors in my life were not considered in her final
diagnosis. There were monumental physical and emotional life stressors beyond the car accident that she
failed to take into account. Thankfully, the insurance
representative appeared to not believe the diagnosis.
They felt it was necessary that I have the information
that was provided to the insurance company changed,
for fear of future repercussions. The agent guided me
through the process, and helped me amend and rec-
oncile the diagnosis to one that was more accurate.

The counseling ordeal was a terrible experience
that my insurance company, my therapist, and my primary care doctor agreed to fight to get changed. Dr.
Chez and Stacia had known me for many years and
knew the diagnosis was incorrect. When I received a

copy of the psychologist's notes and reviewed them, I was horrified at how I was described. I was described as an unsettled woman with inappropriate questioning behavior, extreme paranoia, mistrust, and displaying risky behavior. She listed my moods as varying within the appointment—excitable, upbeat, anxious, and angry. She said I was unstable. The report stated that I was an overweight female with major grandiose behavior and high levels of anxiety. These notes and behaviors were not the real me. Yet, I was going through extreme personality changes, and at the moment—it was the real me.

Many professionals were diligently trying to solve the mystery of the radical differences in my behavior, and yet we could not figure out what had been happening to me since the car accident. Was it the steroids taken from the sinus infection that threw me off? Was I severely dehydrated? Was I having seizures in my sleep? What I not eating well enough? Did I get enough sleep? What was it? We kept trying to figure out how I could return to the person I used to be.

Three months after the car accident, in June, Stacia proposed the idea for me to have a neuropsychological exam. She knew a psychologist, Dr. Towers who worked with many military members. Dr. Towers conducted tests for post-traumatic stress disorder and brain injuries. I was nervous about what the tests might reveal, but I pursed the testing anyway. So many things had been going wrong in my life since the car accident, and I did not have any solutions. One of the hardest parts of the search for solutions was the need to keep these activities secret. If the insurance companies found out about the testing, I would be dropped from my plan. At the time, there were specific diagnoses that would become preexisting conditions and cause me to be ineligible for future health insurance policies. Several mental health professionals cautioned me to be careful about reporting the outcomes of appointments to the health insurance companies. I paid out-of-pocket to keep the results and testing out of the health insurance reporting system. The tests were expensive, and my gracious brothers helped provide the money to obtain the testing I needed. I was so thankful to have their support and assistance in my time of need.

The test began with a twenty-page questionnaire to find facts about the history and status of my health and brain functioning. It was the Amen assessment, which is universally used to understand the history, life-style, and current functioning of an individual. It was an emotionally difficult and time consuming assessment to complete. Various medical histories from family members were needed along with personal experiences, and my memory loss made it even harder to complete. Despite being an exhausting challenge, the assessment was a God-sent solution to help plot my healing.

The bright side of the assessment were all the lifestyle categories it included. There were questions about diet, sleep, daily living, and exercise. The questions became a road map to help heal my brain. It was from this assessment that I learned consuming caffeine and eating pro-cessed foods would not help my brain heal. I did learn that working on my balance through exercise would help my brain heal quicker.

I completed the assessment and started the journey of two days of testing. The neuropsychology tests vary, but many include activities of self-reporting attitudes and beliefs, problem-solving, completing puzzles and visual tests, assessing attention spans, and measuring reaction times. It was my first experience with the Rorschach test beyond reading about it in psychology books. The test is a series of black shapes made out of ink blots on a piece of paper, and the person has to describe what they see. When she showed me the first picture in the Rorschach test and asked me what I saw I answered, "An ink blot." It may not have been an original response, but I used humor as best as I could to cope with the frustration of the testing. There were many aspects of the test I could not complete or I failed at, and humor was my coping mechanism.

During the testing, I could sense my mind was not working correctly. I was unable to correlate simple patterns or spell words, and my responses to sounds were slow. I was not sure if I was experiencing hearing loss from the car accident. When I was asked to complete simple math problems, I was at a loss on how to figure them out. In a memory testing exercise, I was to repeat the words that were spoken in order, and I could only get past the first few words. I struggled simply reading the instructions for the test, because I could not remember what I had read a few moments beforehand. Many aspects of my brain were not functioning correctly. I was growing increasingly agitated as I knew I was failing. It was then that I knew the reality of my situation, and the test results confirmed what I was thinking. I had sustained a traumatic brain injury in the car accident. I never hit my head, but the impact of the jolt in the car accident caused my brain to smash against the front of my skull. I was really starting to understand the full scope of what I could no longer do. I could not spell like I used to. I was not retaining anything I read for a longer span of time, nor could I figure out simple puzzles. The greatest impact appeared to be on my short-term memory and my working memory abilities. The accident left me with a very limited amount of memory, and I was experiencing a great deal of stress, which placed a burden on my brain functioning.

Even during the most difficult times, I made a conscientious decision to carry through the testing. It would have been easier to choose to avoid the testing, but I needed answers. The results were hard to accept. I had spent most of my life studying and working in academia, and I was not sure what I would do next as I lost a lot of my brain functioning. The results left me feeling very uncertain about my future. Unfortunately, this was only the first of many tests.

* * *

Another aspect of the healing journey, to ease the constant headache pain, was to work with a physical therapist. This was to help in repositioning how I carry my neck and shoulders to decrease the headaches. I was pleased to work in a physical therapy center that focused on sports medicine. It was very inspiring to work with the athletes who knew they would get well. They encouraged me and I adopted the mantra that I would get well, too. I must be honest, it was nice to complete physical therapy with so many healthy, fit, and attractive men. At the same time, recall that I was having difficulty keeping my mouth shut and not saying what was really on my mind—that created a dilemma when I was in physical therapy! Regardless of the challenges, physical therapy helped me manage my headaches tremendously.

Following the neuropsychology testing, the psychologist recommended I work with a neuropsychiatrist to create a recovery strategy. I started a new journey of healing and added another professional to the growing team. Dr. Newsome was a leading neuropsychiatrist that worked at several of the well-known Chicago area rehabilitation hospitals, and was currently leading his own brain research institute.

Dr. Newsome recommended some newer tests for my brain, to understand the level of activity and functioning. This allowed us the chance to understand the specific areas of the brain that were most effected by the car accident. I had both the SPECT (single-photon emission computerized tomography) scan and QEEG's (quantitative electroencephalography) testing conducted. The SPECT scan shows the colorful results to display activity and function in the brain. My SPECT scan showed the area majorly impacted by the injury was the frontal lobe, which impacts executive function and short-term memory.

The SPECT scan and the neuropsychological tests confirmed I sustained a traumatic brain injury. The results started to provide an explanation for how and why my behaviors and skills had changed. My short-term memory was very limited. It explained why I could not remember things after I had read them. This also gave me clues as to how to adapt my lifestyle to survive.

What did I need to consider when living with a short-term memory? I had to come up with ways to handle and simplify my daily routines. Mundane things, like creating an exact place for my keys, became extremely important. I hung them on a hook so I wouldn't forget where they were. I also needed to be very specific with list making to help me organize my daily tasks, such as taking my prescription medication.

As I continued to work with the neuropsychiatrist, his first treatment recommendation was holistic. He focused on nutrition and nutraceuticals. We had long conversations on lifestyle behaviors to help improve my brain functioning. The nutraceuticals he recommended were fish oil, Taurine, and 5-HTP to help improve the functions of my brain and my moods. The nutraceuticals proved to be a great alternative route.

The other avenue of testing was to work with QEEG tests. These measure the activity in the brain while taking tests. I am not sure if I felt this really helped much along the way, but we were able to rule out one treatment method. During one of the QEEG sessions, we did a pre- and posttest session along with my taking a dose of Ritalin. The doctor wanted to see if the medication would help improve my focus. In my testing, there was no evidence Ritalin provided any improved functioning of my brain, so it was not part of my treatment plan.

Many times on this healing journey, I felt as though I was tossing darts at the ceiling to see what would stick. There is no clear journey for anyone as they continue to uncover their own specific way to heal from a brain injury. It is similar to working on puzzle without having the cover of the box to see the end result.

Another difficulty in healing from the brain injury was the additional stress that came along with the process. While healing from the brain injury, I was terminated from my professor role at the university. I lost not only my career but also a significant part of my brain functions. I felt so much stress from not being able to function at the same capacity. I wondered if I would ever heal. I still felt as though I was racing through life, surviving on very little sleep. It was at this time of my journey that my mantra "always expect a miracle" needed to become a central focus. I needed God to guide me, and He did.

How I responded in various environments had also changed. I was suddenly highly sensitive and easily startled. This became apparent when I went to the movies with my friends and family. We would not even watch scary movies, but at any remotely startling moment I would jump out of my seat and scream. It became quite embarrassing for my niece and nephews in the movie theatre. I would also experience vertigo or nausea if explosions or fast movements would occur on the large screen, even on videos that were shown at church. I learned it was a change in functioning related to my vagus nerve.

The stress levels of this experience were so high. The significant feelings of loss from my job, my coworkers, and my brain functions were overwhelming. It was recommended by Dr. Newsome to move beyond the nutraceutical approach to get more rest for my brain. He prescribed Seroquel and Pristiq to help with my moods and get more sleep to help my brain heal. Turning into Sleeping Beauty on antidepressants was the next part of my journey. I had heard at the Illinois Brain Injury Conference that many doctors help their brain injury patients by medicating them to sleep. Increasing sleep helps the brain heal faster. What I was unaware of was the total length of time needed to keep a person sleeping.

Initially it was nice to slow down and get rest. I was living my life in much slower motion. What I did not know was how slow it would get, and that all of my emotions would become muted. After a few days on the medication, I was no longer expressive and was often sleeping more than twelve hours a night.

My sleep pattern was to head to bed at 8 p.m. and wake up at 8 a.m. As the medicine worked to help me sleep, my thinking and speaking started to slow down significantly. I developed long pauses between words while I was speaking because I could not think of the next word to say. I could barely tell a story without forgetting something.

Another change was my outward affect. I am a very positive, smiling, and energetic person. On the medication, I kept a straight face with very little emotional expression. I felt as though I had lost some awareness of my entire being. I was numb; I didn't even have feelings. I went from being super expressive to mute. My inability to perceive feelings became clear when our church choir sang during a funeral at church. The person who passed away was a longtime church member who many people loved. It was during the memorial service when I clearly noticed I was numb to my feelings. A very heartfelt story was told about the woman and the entire room was in tears, except me. I was the only one not crying. I was not feeling any emotion at all.

I am generally a happy and positive person and the medications were greatly changing who I was. I was on antidepressants, but a great depression settled in. Sleeping and not wanting to wake up was the pattern for my life. I remember waking up in bed thinking I had nothing to wake up for, and I didn't seem to have a purpose in life. I would stare out the window and watch for the mail truck to drive by, then look at the clock to count how many hours it was until I could go back to sleep.

Depression is extraordinarily hard. The medicines that were supposed to help me were numbing me to life. The sleeping to help my brain was taking over my life. I needed to set an alarm to wake up, even after sleeping nearly twelve hours. I was very bored and could find no joy in my life. Nothing was interesting and nothing motivated me. This time was a very frightening time because I actually wondered if I wanted to live. Sadly, this often occurs with people who have had brain injuries and experience PTSD. I did not have much hope. Thankfully, family, friends, and doctors had full faith I would recover as they all prayed for me. Being put into sleep mode was frightening for me. I had been in sleep mode for about six months and I wondered if my brain had enough time to heal.

One blessing of the entire journey was my own interest in health prevention, wellness, and spirituality. The importance I placed on those aspects truly pulled me through during difficult times. The other blessing that helped me cope with the TBI is that I had an established relationship with my primary care doctor and therapist. The beauty of these relationships in the healing process was that my doctor and therapist could hold in their own minds, a benchmark and memory of who I was before the TBI. This was critically important in working with all the medical and mental health professionals on my road to healing. Stacia and Dr. Chez knew the path to return me to the person I once was. They both were able to discuss their perspectives and ideas to get me the best healing care possible.

Life has not been easy for me since a very young age. My parents suffered early deaths when I was only six years old. Trauma can do a heck of a lot to the physical body, mind, and spirit. I add this to answer the question as to why I have a primary care physician and therapist. They worked with me previously on healing from other issues, such as losing my physical ability to have children. These two professionals were of tremendous support after the car accident. They still remain as two stable health care professionals in my life that support my health and well-being.

Dr. Chez and Stacia were critical pieces in solving the puzzle of my healing. They collaborated together and started to push me out of my depression toward healing and recovery. This was no easy task. Fear of so many things held me back from healing. Would I lose my house? Could I work again? Would I ever be happy again? I felt I had no life purpose, and I was sure healing was not possible.

I am certain God was directing Dr. Chez and Stacia's work, along with many others. God had a plan. One of those plans included His giving me an awareness about my lack of emotions and depression. Looking back, I can easily see the depression, but when I was in the middle of it I could not see it. I was so numb I didn't even consider that I was sick. God used the people in my community to wake me up and give me a new awareness. God and the coaching Dr. Chez and Stacia provided were the affirmations that I could heal. As time passed, conversations were no longer about the past accident and the brain injury. We started talking about issues in the present moment.

Stacia was the first to declare that she no longer saw me in disability status. When I asked her to provide records and evidence for my disability insurance, she would not send the records. Dr. Chez agreed with her, and he also did not see it necessary to supply the records. This effectively took me off disability insurance.

I am certain Dr. Chez and Stacia knew I could heal and pull out of depression. But I had to take some risks and innovate ideas on how I would pull out of depression and get back to work. Again, God had a plan. During one of my appointments with Dr. Chez, he asked if I was sure I needed to be on that much medication from the neuro-psychiatrist. He bluntly stated, "I think you are overmedicated." Huh? It was like I was splashed in the face with a bucket of ice water. It was a turning point for me.

I went back to Stacia to talk about what Dr. Chez said. She, too, agreed that I was overmedicated and needed to drop the psychotropic meds. It was very scary and exciting at the time. This would be no easy task, given the fact that

I was on so many medications. It was time to decide and make a plan.

Given there were so many medical professionals involved in my care, we needed a strategy to work together. What would I be like without medication? Would I still be easy to anger? Would I still feel drunk and uninhibited? Most importantly, could I do it? Together, we needed to convince Dr. Newsome, the neuropsychiatrist, that I need to come off the medications. Weaning off these types of drugs is a challenging task. I would like to say it is as easy as stopping immediately the next day, but it's not. We had to put a plan into place. I needed to learn and focus on all the various ways to support my brain and moods to come off of the medications. First, I remained taking the nutraceuticals to support my mood and improve brain functioning. Second, I took a hard look at my eating habits. What were my best choices to eat well for great brain function? Third, I knew I needed to increase my level of exercise to push more endorphins in my body to boost my mood. Exercise is the greatest antidepressant. Finally, I had to get the courage to make all of these changes. My life depended on it.

I never gave the experience a name, but it seems the

best description is a combination of bravery and faith. What this challenge gave me was a critical vision and goal for healing. My reinvention work was moving forward with my career coach, Joann, and reality set in that I needed to get back to receiving a paycheck and a new career. I had to challenge myself to take this combination approach to move off the medication. In these types of situations, for healing to truly begin, it sometimes requires one of the health professionals to take a stand and say, "It's over! Time to move on." It means shifting the locus of control from being a reactive victim to a proactive, empowered force to be reckoned with. I am not sure how long I would have remained on the high doses of medication if it were not for the courage and faith of Dr. Chez and Stacia to take a stand on moving me off the medication.

The process took some time, for I needed to prove I was stable enough to live my life without the medications. I had to create an exercise routine with a solid nutrition plan. I needed to create a blueprint for my strategy to regain work and improve the clarity of my thinking. Immediately, my blueprint was starting to take shape. I had the career coach process in action. I began implementing physical activity back into my daily routine, eventually taking up bicycling as part of my healing journey. I started a nutrition plan and detoxification process. I slowly rebuilt my communication and interaction skills.

After some time with the blueprint in action, Dr. Chez and Stacia collaborated to discuss my being weaned off the medication. I had two antidepressants to drop off in the process. Together, they supported me and worked with Dr. Newsome to ensure I was on the right path to healing.

As the exercise increased, my moods of happiness increased. While changing my eating habits to understand eating for vitality, my liveliness and thinking improved. When my career planning progressed, my self-determination increased. We had a winning plan. I was ready to move off the medications. It took only a few weeks to wean me off the medications, and it was a success. I know a big reason for the success was the many prayers I had from my family, friends, and church community. I am blessed I was able to progress so far in healing from the traumatic brain injury. I am forever grateful.

The medical aspects of healing from a brain trauma is different for everyone. Part of the puzzle includes lifestyle.

I came into the experience with an existing focus on wellness beliefs, higher education, research skills, and strong faith in God. I learned through this process the many ways to heal.

I invite you to join me further on navigating the RIDE of change to wellness and healing. The following chapters discuss in detail the many dimensions and processes I used to heal from my traumatic brain injury. These processes and ideas can help with recovering from a TBI, but they are also valuable for resiliency and coping to work through other challenges and major life changes.

The Therapy Path

Who needs therapy? Everyone. We are all complex human beings with diverse life experiences, and those experiences shape who we are. In life, it is necessary to have various levels of support for our own well-being. We need different outlets and different opinions to gain alternative ways to view the circumstances we are going through. In times of stress and transition, I find it helpful to work with a therapist. When trouble arises, I need to find ways I can take personal responsibility to make my life better. A therapist helps me evaluate how I think about and perceive different situations. By evaluating a situation, I can make determinations as to where I need to make changes, or if I am pushing my own expectations onto others. Every person needs therapy during their lifetime for a better understanding of one's self, and to move effectively through the tough life situations that we all face at some point.

I started working with my therapist, Stacia, when I was having some challenges dealing with stress related to my job. At that time, she helped me understand how my goal-seeking behavior could be misunderstood by others. I discovered a solution, resolving a lot of strife at work and solidifying her supportive role in my life. Since then, we have worked together on and off for several years. She knows who I am as a person, including all my possibilities and challenges. Stacia was my leadership coach while I was developing a new project at work and experiencing some great advances and successes. I was on my way toward being promoted to the next rank. An assistant professor at the time, my goal was to be promoted to associate professor and gain tenure. It was an exciting time in my career, as I thought I was living my professional dream. But on March 3, 2010, I was rudely awakened from that dream.

I was on my way home from an early morning bible study, planning a quick stop at home before heading into work. Life was normal—but then in the blink of an eye, it wasn't. The car accident took *me* on a ride, forcing me to navigate my way through what unfolded in my personality, way of thinking, physical health, and career. After the accident occurred I tried to move forward as if nothing happened. But something had changed—me.

One of the first losses in my career was my dignity. The complete meltdown I had during the American Society of Aging Conference forced me to leave early and left me feeling unprofessional. I was not making sense when I left, and I needed to have a cab take me to my home in the suburbs. I was embarrassed and felt shame. Yes, everyone has challenges, but I was distraught that my lack of coherency was on the other side of such great success with the Positive Aging Conference. It was a bit ironic that I was experiencing so many difficulties with my thinking, a symptom that often occurs when an older person experiences the onset of dementia or Alzheimer's. My meltdown left me feeling humiliated and confused about returning to work. I was starting to feel apprehensive about my job and stressed about the changes in my behavior. I was able to take time off from work thanks to the FMLA, and I tried to manage myself back to wellness. I was very blessed to have over ten years of full-time work experience at the college and the ability to take paid medical leave time to heal and recover. My focus was on healing and not work. My personality was changing though, and I was having difficulty coping.

I was on medical leave to figure out my physical condition. My daily priorities shifted from work to medical appointments. It was difficult to cope with the uncertainties of my condition, and stepping away from work when it appeared to be going so well was tough for me as well. So my initial therapy sessions with Stacia focused on stress management and healing, mainly how to manage my medical issues. I needed to employ new strategies to handle stress and cope with my changes in life. I was blessed that Stacia was part of a larger network of wellness professionals, and the center she worked at offered many healing and wellness classes that I took advantage of.

Stacia has training in dance movement therapy along with her social work credential. I had time on my hands because I wasn't working, so it was natural for Stacia to recommend a Middle Eastern dance class that was being offered at her center. It was a great way to work on my healing and stress reduction. The music was therapeutic and the body movements were great for my brain. It also helped me reestablish a sense of community. Not working had left me missing my colleagues and a sense of meaning and purpose in my life. It felt weird to not be at work, taking time to do fun, stress-relieving activities while others were working. I posted a photo on Facebook of me in a painting class, and one of my co-workers was confused because she knew I was on medical leave. Sharing on social media the fun activities I was doing was challenging, because people questioned whether or not I was actually sick. TBI's are an invisible health problem.

Stacia helped me focus on the healing to return to work. As time progressed, she continued to be a strong resource to help direct my healing. Stacia recommended many holistic techniques, such as nutrition, exercise, and spirituality, to explore as we looked for answers in the early part of the journey following the car accident. She guided me in many ways to full restoration. The majority of my journey with Stacia related to the changes of my own identity. Before the accident, I had a solid identity as a successful college professor and pioneer in the positive aging movement. I was breaking new territory and gaining notoriety until it all stopped on that fateful day in March. I thought I had control of my career path, but I watched it unravel in a few short months and it was devastating at times. I was so blessed to have Stacia's guidance on my road to recovery.

* * *

In May, I was released by Dr. Chez to return to work. I still had tremendous headaches, but I was managing life a lot better. I was excited to return to work and to teach again. I rejoined the staff and had a wonderful time teaching an interpersonal communications class.

It was great to be back with everyone and working again. Yet something was not right. I was experiencing some forgetfulness. My bubbly personality had turned into sassy and aggressive. I thought perhaps it was a result of being in constant pain from the headaches. I became more opinionated and vocal in meetings, taking strong stances on issues and speaking out boldly. I took my concerns to some of the higher-ups, which did not help my career. The changes in my work personality led me to receive a recommendation from one of the deans to return to medical leave, and a referral to the Employee Assistance Program (EAP) for job coaching and behavioral modification. I was devastated.

Stacia continued to coach me on many levels related to working, managing stress, and healing. She helped me look at the many stressors in my life, and asked me to create step-by-step goals for each stressor. I had to evaluate the level of my ability to take action or not, which helped me create action plans. We reached a point where she recommended I see a psychologist who specialized in military personnel who were healing from traumatic brain injuries to find out if I could possibly have a traumatic brain injury. We were still navigating the unknown of the problems I was experiencing, seeking any means to find answers. I was working with the EAP and following through on other recommendations from my employer for about a month after being placed on medical leave for the second time. The challenges at work continued, and I was fired the very same day I was diagnosed with a traumatic brain injury.

I had put in many successful years as a professor and could not believe I was terminated. I was fired for a claim of insubordination, but I thought it was truly a misunderstanding and miscommunication. My beliefs were later confirmed in a review of the situation with the Illinois Department of Employment Security. Stacia helped me navigate the many stages of loss and transition from this drastic change. The process to fully recover from being terminated from my job took years. Going from professor to zero was hard to accept, considering I was a dedicated career woman. I was humiliated and angry. I felt cheated and threatened. I thought it was unfair and wrong, but none of that mattered to anyone else. I was fired, period. Over time I learned that many folks get fired, life does return to normal, and people do survive.

In loss and grieving there is a process that includes denial, anger, bargaining, depression, and acceptance. All of these steps are equally difficult, and thankfully, Stacia helped me move through each of them.

I denied so much that had happened and that it even could happen. I was processing so many thoughts about my positive contributions to the college, and could not believe my work was no longer valued. It boggled my mind that my colleagues would turn against me after so many years of friendship. I did not think the questions I had asked about my work were grounds for termination. I was in denial for several months. I kept fighting their decisions in my head. I finally snapped out of it when I started to realize the many things I had lost in the firing. Plus, a delivery truck came with ten boxes full of my office belongings. I could no longer deny it.

The hardest part was working through anger. I was angry at the college for firing me. I was angry at myself for the car accident. I was mad about the conflicts that occurred at work and decisions I made that led to my termination. I was angry at myself for investing so much of my identity into a career that without it, I thought I was nothing. I was so frustrated and needed to find ways to channel my anger. I took the recommendation of a friend to beat a pillow with a tennis racket. It actually helped me shift my focus and shake the anger feelings out of my body. I also spent a lot of time writing to work through my thoughts and feelings of anger. I would write letters to the people I felt anger towards, and then I would burn them. Frankly, I eventually got tired of being angry. One of my friends finally asked, "What would happen if you focused your anger on your healing? Wouldn't that make more sense?" I couldn't argue, it was a great idea!

I tried my hand at bargaining the situation, thinking I could get my job back once they knew I had a documented brain injury. I asked my doctors to write letters with compelling reasons as to why I deserved to get my job back. I kept talking to people who knew me and my character, hoping they would remember who I was before the accident and ask me back to work. I also bargained with God. I asked God every night in my prayers for my return to the professor position and my role as director. I could not understand the loss, for I thought I had been doing a great job.

One of the toughest parts of grieving any loss is that everyone goes through a different process. I had to get to a point of being able to let go, so that I could move forward. Several legal issues and clarifications about my unemployment needed to be resolved, but it was taking months, making my situation more challenging. These connections kept me stuck in the grieving process and slowed my healing. I finally surrendered to many of the work-related challenges in November, and chose to focus fully on my personal healing.

Stacia greatly helped me process the loss, grieving, and sadness. It was a scary place not knowing who I was in terms of my own identity. It was also difficult not knowing what would happen in my future. I learned it was necessary to take one day at a time—heal first, then build what is next. Stacia supported me as I went through debilitating depression. I showed up every week, barely crawling out of bed, certain my life was slipping away. I did not find anything interesting, engaging, or important. There were times I lost hope and lacked emotion because I was so overly medicated. The medication slowed me down tremendously, which is so different from who I usually am. I did not have much to fill my days with, except medical appointments and sleep. I was sleeping so much my body was getting very lethargic. I would wake up not feeling rested, and I really had no purpose motivating me to become more active. Stacia recommended that I should try to do things I loved, but I had no interest. I did not want to go anywhere. I did not want to see anyone. I often stayed in my house for several days in a row, never bothering to get out of my pajamas. I felt I had lost my life's purpose, which contributed to my major depression. I desperately needed change.

Stacia's expertise in dance movement therapy was beneficial in helping regain my strength and brain functionality, and she also knew that I just needed to physically *move*. There are many ways to heal the brain, and one way is through intentional movement of both sides of the body. Stacia taught me body movements that helped me rebuild my balance and establish new pathways in my brain. Each week we would spend some of our time in movement. In an exercise called womping, I was able to experience part of the movements from a practice called Brain Gym. Brain Gym involves specific movements to help activate brain activity and increase focus. I found these movements to be very helpful. We also worked on motion in the dimensional scale, which is movement that crosses both sides of the body to create pathways across both sides of the brain. These intentional movements were pivotal exercises that allowed me to regain my balance and awaken my brain.

* * *

In William Bridges work on transition, he speaks of three phases of transition: the ending, the unknown or neutral zone, and a new beginning. I was simultaneously processing through many endings, sitting in the unknown, and struggling to find a new beginning. Each one of these phases comes with a variety of emotions and actions, and Stacia was there to help me navigate my way through all of the transitions.

The ending phase usually encompasses elements of shock, denial, and anger. This was very true in my experience. I was in complete shock about losing so much from the car accident. Stacia worked to help me see that even though I was suffering many losses, I still had many other positives in my life.

The neutral zone has aspects of frustration, apathy, confusion, and listlessness. For me, the neutral zone was the most difficult aspect of the entire transition. I did not know who I was, I did not know what to do with my time, and I could not see any path to follow. This, too, was a difficult time for Stacia to work with me. She was most concerned about my depression, and there was not much for me to report when I did not have much going on in my life. I did not see or have much hope.

Once I was able to see a vision for my life I was in the phase of new beginnings, filled with excitement and high energy. I was able to redefine my life, and that was exhilarating. The new beginnings continued to rise as I did more movement and positive actions to foster change in my life. Stacia was a great cheerleader who helped me move toward my new goals.

After months of therapy, the time came where I knew I could no longer stay on disability and I needed to move forward. But I was completely unmotivated and felt worthless. Looking back, I realize I was in the unknown phase of transition, uncertain of my own brain capacity and ability to progress. Stacia stuck by me the entire time to assist me in moving through this difficult period. What would I do next for work? Who would be my new community? Who was I as a person? It was an unknown factor, or as some might say, a blank canvas from which to create. Stacia had a multitude of resources and she recommended I work with a career coach.

To be honest, I was fearful and had no desire to work with the career coach, Joann. She had been a successful career coach with great results, but I was still scared. Stacia encouraged me and helped me work through those emotions. Stacia and Joann soon became my new transformation team, geared toward moving me forward to return to work. Joann had a great process that helped me walk through an initial assessment of my career status to determine what my career reentry plan would be. There was quite a bit of balancing in relearning my career skills and rebuilding my professional identity. Who was I? I certainly looked great on a resume, but I was entirely unsure of what my brain could handle. I had, it seemed, endless work experience, but I wondered if I could do it again. Stacia was instrumental in helping me regain my confidence. She reassured me that I had learned it all once and I could do it again. She helped me rebuild my communication skills and identity one step at a time.

Joann challenged me to go networking, which absolutely terrified me. Networking was not the very first activity I tried because I needed to work up my confidence to get to those events. I had to get reacquainted with my community to reestablish old friendships and make new ones. Instead, my first challenge was to take a class somewhere. It could be any topic of my choosing, but it had to help me get more connected to people and my community. I selected a yoga class as my reentry, and it really did help me feel like part of a group again. Stacia coached me along the way, constantly encouraging me to step out of my shell. I built up the confidence to attend a non-profit fair in the city of Chicago after a month of working with Joann. It was an extreme challenge for me. It would be my first large-scale networking event, and my first time driving downtown since the disaster at the aging conference. I mustered up every ounce of courage and persevered. I felt much stronger and more confident after I completed that first networking event, and it became easier to get involved in more activities and events.

* * *

Stacia helped me work through my emotions and thought processes throughout the building of my new identity. I should clarify that I am not a completely different person, but so much of who I was had changed. Because Stacia has known me for such a long time, it was natural for her to help me bring back some of my old self and let go of things that no longer served me. She was an excellent cheerleader and a pillar of strength. She continued to affirm that my brain *would* heal and all would return to normal. It would be a new normal, and perhaps an even better normal. Stacia continued to help me create a new vision for my life, and she gave me hope on some of my darkest days.

I left so much emotional baggage behind in the car accident, and this journey allowed me to be honest with my life. It was a shift in my mind-set related to my past, and it turned out to be relevant to all of my past. My brain certainly changed from the accident as older memories did not seem to hurt any more. Things that had once weighed me down suddenly seemed trivial. In the new beginning phase of my transformation, I had the chance to focus on and rediscover what I loved doing and who I was. I realized that, perhaps, my old job was not the best place for me. I had a blank canvas—carte blanche—to create my entire life. I looked forward to grabbing the paint and creating a new vision, a new way of being.

A big part of Stacia's influence was working on my fears. I was scared I would lose my home. I was terrified about money, and my greatest concern as a single woman was losing my job. Of course my financial fears were piled on top of all of my other fears surrounding the accident and brain injury. Needless to say, I had a lot to work on in the fear department. Stacia continued to be resourceful. When I felt I was running out of money, she recommended seeking assistance from food pantries. We talked over money strategies and financial planning, which helped me work through the stress and fear. There were so many what-if scenarios causing me fear. What if I lost my home? What if I could not read and retain information again? What if I were hurt again emotionally, like when I was fired? What if I could never trust again? It was the many false fears that kept me stuck. Throughout this journey, I have learned that fear can be transformed into false expectations that only appear to be real. I learned to question fears and face them directly.

Many times on the journey, I needed to recreate my mind-set. An important psychological aspect Stacia helped me with was getting over feeling like a victim. The victim mind-set is very common, and it kept me in a disempowered state. I was a victim and helpless, but I had to move forward. Conquering a victim state of mind is difficult. Stacia challenged me to take a look at my own locus of control. In a victim state, I gave my control and power to someone else. To progress in my healing I needed to regain command and take charge of my life. Stacia helped me move from being a *victim* of a car accident, a traumatic brain injury, and job loss, to a *victor* of new beginnings, complete healing, and new work opportunities.

Stacia helped me work through the entire experience of my traumatic brain injury from start to finish. It was a transformation, a rebuild. She walked me through grief, depression, hopelessness, and into the joy of the re-creation of my life. Brain injury experiences are different for every person. I found, in working on mental wellness, the most important factor was to have a stable advocate on my team. My steadfast champion was my therapist, Stacia.

The Career Coach Path

It was April 2011. A year had passed since my car accident, and it was time to focus on how I would rejoin the workforce. I had applied to Social Security to claim disability status, but was denied. What on earth would I do as a person who was recovering from a brain injury and previously fired as a professor? This was the ultimate question to answer.

Unemployment and my disability insurance were running out. I was unable to unlock any of my retirement funds. Medical bills and prescription costs continued to accrue and I needed solutions. I was becoming more afraid by the day, and I did not know where to turn. What's next? I wondered.

After much coaxing and convincing, my therapist encouraged me to set up an appointment with a career coach. It was very scary, as I felt I had lost all my skills and abilities in the accident. Who was I anyway? I struggled to know who I had become as a person and as a professional worker. My therapist gave me a recommendation to a local career coach and encouraged me to make an appointment.

That April I took my first steps to regain a working career through my initial assessment with Joann, the career coach. I felt so lost and ashamed for being fired from my wonderful professor position. I thought I would never recover. I was not sure who to "be" at this point, as I was not clear I wanted, or even *could,* return to being a college professor again. I wondered if I had the brain capacity to be a college professor. Additionally, given what I learned about higher education in my last position, I wasn't sure I wanted to return to that type of organizational culture. I was puzzled about what I would do to pay my bills and create a career.

The journey of working with a career coach intimidated me because I really wasn't sure how my brain would work. I was no longer in the usual pattern of working in today's fast-paced life with a constant flow of incoming emails and phone calls. My life, being in a healing phase, had become very quiet and included a limited number of people. Would my brain be able to handle the capacity of communication necessary to survive in today's workforce?

When I lost my position as a professor I lost all my colleagues at that institution. There were also other roles I lost in various professional organizations because I was no longer an educator. My behavior was erratic and unstable with all the stress and the changes in my personality from the brain injury. It was a frightening and unsettling time due to the nature of the conflict with my administrative leave and termination. I had restricted communication with anyone at the college—it was *nineteen years* of lost friendships and colleagues. It was not only a loss of my career but also all the colleagues and people I believed to be friends. People did not want to associate with me because I had changed so much, and because the conflict at the school was difficult, many avoided me until it was all settled. The brain injury may have come with with psychological problems, but it felt as though I had leprosy. These feelings can happen when someone is unemployed because our society tends to focus a person's identity on his or her work. My identity was so wrapped up in my career that it was pure anxiety planning what persona I would create next.

I felt hopeless during the initial intake assessment

when I met with my career coach for the first time. We had several tasks ahead. We had to determine what resources I needed to launch a new career, and reestablish an understanding of my talents and skills to rebuild a career. When I walked into the first session I had no idea where I wanted to go with my career next. I didn't even know what was possible because I did not fully understand the condition of my brain. I also continued to be on very heavy doses of anti-depression medication, which was very concerning to me. My thinking and speaking were slow. Despite these obstacles, each week I started to experience more hope as I reviewed my work history and other skills.

The first part of my career reinvention was to let go of the past. I was given a writing prompt to help me work through my feelings and thoughts about my last job. I wrote about the things I loved, and I wrote about the things I hated. I was able to dissect the troublesome situation and professional network, and separate the experiences that were positive. In the end, I had the chance to embrace all I had learned from the job I lost. I was able to assess both the good and the bad of the situation as life lessons.

The writing about my past work challenges was a journey in letting go, forgiving myself and others, and a redemption of who I was in the world of work. Honestly, we tried to reach the full redemption and forgiveness parts, but those took time. I had a lot of grieving yet to experience. The biggest part was to work through the shame. I had to forgive myself for my behavior, even though I was dealing with a traumatic brain injury. I did not have much executive brain function, which helps filter and control behavior. The journey to heal took time. The ending of my job writing prompt was a great start to a lot of new opportunities.

The next phase of working through my career coach's process included assessing my skills and experiences. What does a person do with twenty years of college teaching and ten years of training, training management, and consulting when they are unsure if they want to continue on that path? The best advice I received was to take an assessment called the Motivated Skills Inventory, which can be found online. It is an amazing assessment that helped me figure out the skills I have and the skills I really love. When those two are combined it makes work much easier. With my many job and life experiences, it was hard to decide what to focus on first. Should I go for a teaching role? Should I head back to training with the military? Should I start all over and chart a new career path?

I spent many career sessions with my career coach talking through my job history to understand the highlights and lowlights. We talked about career aspirations I had, and times when they were sidetracked. It was encouraging to document all the various skills I had during my career. We included conversations about my vast volunteer experiences. We also spent time discussing any other interests I might want to pursue. I had so many experiences it was overwhelming. We had to figure out a way to narrow and focus.

My coach recommended taking the outcomes of the Motivated Skills Inventory and describing each term with my own definitions. I had to rank each of the items in order of what I liked best. The challenge of the assessment was to narrow down the many skills and activities to only five. I had so much work experience it proved to be difficult. There were multiple skills that I could perform well.

The second part of the assessment had me look at the skills in which I found the most delight using. I had to find what tasks were energizing me at work and what were potentially draining me. The final part of the assessment compared the two groups, what I could perform well at and what I had the most delight in using. When I compared and prioritized the skills, these became my motivated skills. It was a combination of what was easy to do and what I really liked to do. The assessment helped me concentrate on what brought me the most happiness. My true motivated skills turned out to be teach, train, perform, counsel, and portray images. Now I had to determine what it all meant to me.

Joann, my career coach, encouraged me to provide meaning to those words. I had to define my motivated skills from my own perspective. For example, to me, portraying images is related to my photography, but it was also a definition of my ability to cast a vision in leading others. When speaking about teaching, I viewed it as training, and not solely in a traditional educational setting. The counsel skill was related to encouraging, coaching, and guiding people on their paths, rather than just professional counseling. My perform skill was related to my professional motivational and leadership speaking engagements.

The most important part of starting this exercise was to help me regain focus. It helped me make a decision to pursue work only in my most highly motivated skills. I was overwhelmed in not knowing who I was in the work world, so prioritizing the skills provided me with a baseline for a new career direction.

I reinvented my career by using the completed Motivated Skills Inventory and a focusing on my greatest skills. This helped me as I completed other assessments and writing prompts to further describe what I wanted in my career reinvention. My coach guided me to assess my past roles, personal interests, career values, and industries. I am certain this sounds easier than the actual process. The journey was truly an exercise in soul-searching. I had to answer hard questions, such as when I would choose money over happiness and position authority over my personal life. It gave me the chance to review the successes and the mistakes on my career path. It was affirming, but humbling at the same time.

In the twists and turns of the career review, I was highly critical. I felt like a complete failure after being fired. I discovered many instances where my ego, rather than my common sense, led my career actions. There were many insights and areas of growth. The key part of my growth was to learn more about what my brain could and could not do. I worked with Joann for several sessions before she admitted she knew me from my previous work role. She had been a guest expert at one of our public education events. I was embarrassed that I did not recognize her at first, but the memory of her returned as my brain became better at recalling the most recent past.

Before the accident, I was a full-time professor in behavioral sciences and the director of the Center for Positive Aging, which I had designed. I felt I had my dream career. I was on top of the world. I had amazing colleagues all over the country to work with to bring my new retirement agenda forward. The new retirement research I was doing was part of my original doctoral research and the design for the Center for Positive Aging. Our identity and leadership is always in constant motion. The moment I lost my position, my phone stopped ringing and the emails stopped coming. The change of influence diminished my self-concept and self-esteem. Self-concept is a combination of ideas about one's self and the ideas others have about us. No title, no job, and I was nothing. Those thoughts were a hard blow to my self-esteem, but just ahead of me was a redesign of who I was beyond my career.

I was in a solid series of difficult experiences, and I needed to take a major dose of self-forgiveness, along with a shower of grace. I had to move from victimhood to empowerment. I had taught this theory many times in my classroom before, but how would I make the transition? I was fired and it was natural to feel like a victim. I was suffering from a traumatic brain injury and they still fired me, reinforcing my feelings of injustice. However, there was a way to turn the perspective around. What if there was a higher purpose for these challenges? What could I do now that I was no longer in pursuit of a tenured professor role? What new opportunities would arise? Was hope around the corner? I had to hone in on my own ability to rebuild and redesign my career. I made the choice to move away from being a college professor and opt for a new direction.

One aspect of my career and education that I always loved was the area of health and wellness. In college I minored in public health, and the health field fascinated me. I had the chance to work in the health, wellness, and empowerment field when I worked with the US Navy. I was on a contracted project for about ten years, working on internal locus of control regarding healthy lifestyles. I enjoyed assisting others design their own wellness pathways. I was able to develop and maintain a healthy lifestyle that helped me endure difficult life situations. I enjoyed my previous work with health and wellness immensely, so in this career break I had the chance to explore the field further. In my undergraduate degree work I learned about the importance of focusing on the wellness wheel. This balanced approach to living called for engagement in physical, intellectual, social, spiritual, occupational, emotional, and environmental aspects. As part of my new career path and lifestyle, I decided to obtain a certificate in worksite wellness from the National Wellness Institute. This was one of the career directions that continues to influence my lifestyle and career.

I continued to work with Joann, slowly creating a new path. Another avenue I realized I wanted to explore was to work as a leader in a Fortune 500 company. I had completed my doctoral degrees while I was working in academia, and I felt work experience in corporate America would advance my future career. It was the only element missing from my professional portfolio.

I forged ahead with Joann's guidance and the intense career evaluation, working to redesign my resume. I was planning to change my career course and venture out of higher education. I created several resumes for the various industries and positions possible for my next career move. I worked hard to change my lingo to match the various fields of health, wellness, and business.

A big part of working with my career coach was to reenter new environments and make new job connections. My world had become very small with my family, close friends, and church family, compared to the large professional network I had when I was working. I had to relearn how to be outgoing and conversational. Part of this aspect of my life had fallen apart because of the prescription medications that slowed my thinking and speaking abilities. When speaking, I would often find myself at a loss for words. I would start a sentence, but have to stop to process and look for the next words. It delayed my speech. Even close friends found it hard to speak to me. It broke my confidence and I greatly needed to rebuild my speaking and thinking skills to get back into the work force.

Joann advocated for me to get involved in the community by taking a class at the park district. This would engage my brain and force me to speak with other people. I started with a yoga class at the park district, which improved my stress management and helped my balance and brain. The next challenge was to start networking at local job clubs. This led to my learning more about informational interviewing in new career fields. Informational interviewing is a technique to meet with people to explore their career journeys, and understand a new industry. It is a way to gather information to learn more about possible career paths. I started attending professional association meetings to reconnect with the updated terminology in my fields of interest. The social support built in these groups helped relaunch my career and grow a new professional network.

It is hard to make complete industry jumps in a career, so I needed to adjust my strategy. I had the most experience in higher education, but longed for more business experience to build my credentials. I conducted many informational interviews with recruiters at corporations to understand the jobs available and the business. The best guidance I received was to work in businesses that catered to higher education. This greatly narrowed my search and gave me direction.

It took many months to refine and redesign my career path. After eight months of working with my career coach, I landed my first Fortune 500 leadership role in an organization that partnered with higher education institutions. The role came with many of my top motivated skills—teach, train, counsel, and perform—all wrapped up into the title of market manager. I took the leap of faith and returned to working full time exactly one year and eight months after the car accident. My brain was ready to work again. I had the wonderful experience of working in a fast-paced corporate environment to solidify and validate my doctoral work in management, leadership, and organizational change. Being a Fortune 500 leader was a great experience to build my skill set. This role eventually led to an opportunity to return to college teaching on a part-time basis in the business psychology department at The Chicago School of Professional Psychology. I also returned to teaching at Webster University, in the graduate programs in business and human resources.

The journey I took allowed me to further explore what my true calling in life is. I was previously working within a behavioral science and counseling discipline, forcing me to place my business experiences on hold. What emerged through working with my career coach were the gifts I was truly called to use.

The Nutrition Path

My journey started out very confusing because I did not have a proper diagnosis of what was happening after the car accident. I was not sure what was causing the headaches or the changes in my personality. My neurologist prescribed Topomax for my headaches. Topomax is a drug that is taken daily to prevent migraines. One side effect from the drug that I experienced was a significant loss of appetite. I did not feel hungry, so I did not eat. To make matters worse, because of my short-term memory loss, there were times I could not even remember if I had eaten. I lost about thirty pounds from not eating. The medicine may have been good for headaches and weight loss, but it certainly was not good for my brain.

As I continued to search for ways of getting rid of the

headaches and restoring my brain function, one of the next logical steps was to ensure I was on the right medication to help me heal. Navigating the medicine was challenging because at the time I was still suffering from major headaches and anxiety from being let go from my job. One path I took was to rely on nutraceuticals, or intense-grade supplements. This was a step in the right direction to feed my brain and heal it, too. The first addition was omega fish oils, which are the brain-boosting, cholesterol-clearing good fats. Omega fats help with brain functioning and restoration. I opted for a high-grade EPA-DHA 720 Omega-3 fish oil by Metagenics. Another supplement I added was Taurine by Biotics Research. Taurine is an amino acid that helps with improving mental performance. The third supplement, Neuro 5-HTP Plus by Biotics Research, was to help with moods and depression. It took a few weeks for me to start noticing the impact of the supplements. My thinking became more focused, and my moods were more stable. The key impacts of the supplements were increased memory and overall brain function. These were all positive additions for me.

When I thought back to the Amen assessment I took, I remembered the dietary questions related to everyday living. I used these questions to help me figure out what was good for my brain and what was not good. One simple step I took that certainly helped my brain functioning was to eliminate alcohol and caffeine. They were not beneficial in helping my brain function, and I needed to stop consuming them immediately. I never drank alcohol in excess, but even the smallest amount would impair my thinking further and cause dehydration. I needed as much water as possible to keep my brain healthy.

My caffeine intake was another habit to change. Caffeine has varying effects on people. It was not positive for me, as it caused me to be more anxious and aggressive, obviously not helping my altered personality. Studies do vary on the health benefits, especially of coffee. In 2015 the Journal of Alzheimer's Disease reported mild cognitive impairment over time as an individual consumes more than one cup of coffee per day. There are studies that support the positive benefits of coffee for health and the brain, but the longevity studies from 2015 contradict the positive benefits. In any event, the stimulant did not improve my brain function. The removal of alcohol and caffeine from my diet were both good decisions to help heal my brain.

As I mentioned earlier, the Topomax decreased my appetite, and combined with my short-term memory loss, my eating habits were very poor. When depression starting sinking in, eating was no longer a priority. I was also terrified I would lose my home, so I chose to eat very little in hopes of saving money. Previously I had loved to cook, but because of all I was dealing with, I no longer wanted anything to do with cooking. A typical dinner was five pizza rolls or some chicken and rice. My interest in food was so minimal that heading to the grocery store was a daunting task. I would stand in the aisle dazed, unsure of what food to buy since I had slowed thinking and no appetite. The food we eat is fuel for the mind and body; my brain and body desperately needed some beneficial fuel. My diet had to change in order for me to progress.

As I pulled through the depression, other areas of my life started to gain more energy, and with that my eating improved. I started to become more conscious of what I was eating, and I returned to review the Amen assessment for guidance. When my primary doctor and Stacia decided to take a look at the prescriptions I was taking and make the change to move me off of the medications, it was time to clear out my entire system and do a reset. I first had to build up the courage to make the decision for change, then I needed a lot of support and affirmation that I could do it.

I began the journey to improve my nutrition by talking with some chiropractor friends who had a lot of knowledge about nutrition. Seeking their advice was a start to gain education and make a plan for change. I also had the chance to enroll in a course called Beyond Fitness, which is a part of the Landmark Education seminar series. This class took a holistic approach to all areas of fitness, including nutrition. Additionally, I decided to work with a chiropractor at the Center for Metabolic Disorders. We came up with a plan to help detoxify my body from all of the medication. The process would also help me understand what foods were best for me and my brain health. The questions from the Amen assessment helped me seek out the very best foods for my brain and for detoxification. The Center for Metabolic Disorders hosted sessions to learn more about how to lead a different lifestyle with healthier eating and improved nutrition. I eagerly took their classes, and soon learned they recommended the removal of all processed foods, dairy, and most sugars.

These sessions were my introduction to clean eating.

The program started with thirty days of clean eating and drinking more water. It included the removal of all food and drink items that were known to cause inflammation in the body. It was also designed to help improve digestion. The program was loaded with many whole foods that were healthy for the brain. Going through the program helped me become very intentional about my eating habits. I had to take notes about how I felt if I ate certain foods. This helped me find out what foods gave me better vitality and energy. As the program progressed, I was able to slowly reintroduce some foods back into my diet to determine what was most healthy for me. This gave me the opportunity to find out what food sensitivities might affect me. The foods eliminated were foods that cause many people to have difficulty digesting or experience inflammation. I found out I had a sensitivity to dairy, so I began using almond milk as a substitute.

Of course, my goal was to detox and continue to be headache free. A major shift for me was focusing on hydration. I loved diet coke and coffee, but the main problem with these drinks is the caffeine. Although they are beverages, these two drinks worked against me and worsened my dehydration. Dehydration can be tricky as it is often the cause of headaches, fatigue, irritability, and many other symptoms we might not even think to associate with water. My solution was to focus further on consuming un-caffeinated drinks, most specifically water. As my lifestyle changed with improved nutrition, I followed the recommendation to add lemon into my water to help with digestion and detoxification of my liver. Over time, water became my drink of choice.

The lifestyle change through the clean eating program encouraged me to drop all processed foods, dairy, many seasonings, and sugars from my diet. The goal was to give my body a break from the difficult digestion of processed foods. I continued to increase the amount of vegetables and fruits I ate. I also took a digestive enzyme that helped my body break down protein, allowing for better nutrient absorption. As time progressed, I felt better and achieved more vitality from the natural foods.

Through clean eating, my thinking became clearer and I was able to focus much longer. The process helped me understand better food choices for my brain, health, and overall wellness. I learned more about food nutrition to help my body, and most importantly, my brain functioning. It taught me how to care for my brain and my body in order to recover. On my journey to brain health and restoration, I needed to know and understand that what I was feeding my brain directly impacted my thinking. I learned to include brain healthy foods in my diet every day. Some of my favorite foods that are great for the brain are blueberries, nuts and seeds, avocados, coconuts, and wild salmon.

The better we feed our bodies, the better our brain will be. Our brain is an ever-changing organ and it's always a good time to change your nutrition for the better. I challenge you to track what you are eating for a week by keeping a food diary. At the end of the week, review how much food you ate for your brain. Making a conscious effort to record what you eat increases the likelihood that you will improve your diet. Eating brain healthy foods will have immediate benefits, and will also pay off in the long run. It is never too late to start eating better for your brain.

The Physical Path

Work or play? Although I have always been an advocate for wellness, there were many times that I dedicated more effort to work, in hopes of becoming more successful, rather than making time for physical activity. It was a bargain I was making as I was growing my career. This negotiation came to a halt the day I had the car accident and sustained a traumatic brain injury.

Life did get turned upside down when I had to set down my work to go on medical leave to heal. Initially I did not know it was for a traumatic brain injury, and my doctors and I were just focusing on the incredible headaches. While on leave, my goal was to heal. My life focused on my medical and physical therapy appointments—my new job was to be a patient.

The headaches were intense and we were looking for solutions. I did work with a chiropractor for a while until my primary care doctor, Dr. Chez, prescribed physical therapy. The goal was to help with the soft tissue damage in my neck after the accident. Physical therapy gave me a place to be three times a week, and it also gave me a goal. The goal was to get rid of the headaches. My doctor selected a great physical therapy place. It was a sports related physical therapy center that was very committed to getting people back to their active lifestyles. The focus areas of my physical therapy were to increase mobility in my neck and to rebuild my posture to decrease the headaches. The physical exercises also helped with the reduction of stress.

The beautiful part of the therapy was the community of people working side by side to heal. I continued with physical therapy for six weeks. We worked on neck mobility and then on rebuilding my balance, which was important for my brain and my healing journey. The best part of working with the physical therapy team was their attitude of encouragement. I always knew I would heal, the opposite was not an option, and their ongoing support was tremendous. It was bittersweet when I finished this therapy because I missed the group of people that served as my community.

In the early stages of the injury, I also had time to attend a Middle Eastern dance class. The music was soothing and helped keep my focus and presence in the moment. The more I focused on the present, the less stressed I became. The dancing built new neuropathways in my brain and helped build my balance. In the class I was able to connect with a new community, which helped rebuild my self-esteem. The dancing made me very happy and full of joy. It was a blessing that allowed me to forget about all of my troubles for that one hour of dance.

The physical therapy and dancing were very good for my brain, and they helped me heal tremendously. I participated in these activities before I was placed on the extra medications to help my brain sleep. However, these movements and actions were beneficial in my path to recovery. Physical activity and movement are critical for your body and brain. When we engage more of our body, we engage more of our brain. Physical activity is often overlooked in a passive society that is glued to watching TV or playing video games to relax. It is important to realize that physical activity can also promote relaxation.

When I started taking the extra prescription medications

to help me sleep, I became very lethargic. I did not want to move. My world became very quiet, as watching TV or movies would often trigger a headache or nausea from the flickering lights of the screen. The more I stayed still, the more lethargic I became. I was moving in slow motion. It was during this time that my therapist Stacia started working with me on movement. Some of the exercises she led me in were to express my emotions through movement. I was not experiencing many emotions while on the medication, but the movement helped me understand my feelings on a deeper level. For instance, I would move into positions that would replicate the experience of sad or of happy. I had to create a body movement for the emotions I wanted to embody.

Stacia spent time to teach me movements and exercises to help awaken my brain and body. We did movements that worked on both sides of the body to help cross the left and right hemispheres of the brain. This type of movement is based on the Laban dimensional scales. The movements in this technique include upward, downward, and cross-body motions. Through these exercises we were able to see which side of my brain was working well or was slightly off that day. This would vary every day. The goal of using this method was twofold in working to regain my balance and improve my brain activity. The cross-body techniques created cross-brain communication and healing. When I was not working with Stacia, I would work through the dimensional scales on simple routines to help rebuild my brain. She also had me work on a brain gym routine called womping to activate various parts of my brain through movement. Womping consists of an increase in water and oxygen, in addition to marching and forming the body into a pretzel shape by crossing the arms and legs. The purpose is to help wake up the brain.

At first I was a slow starter and highly unmotivated. A simple trip to the store wore me out. I needed to stop sleeping so much and get into action. Stacia and Joann, my career coach, collaborated and encouraged me to take my first steps. They thought I need to start with something I loved to do, which led me to a yoga class. I took my very first yoga class back when I was in college, and I fell in love with the practice. Yoga is very good for your brain. Beyond the beneficial stretching, yoga activity helps you with balance and keeps you in the present moment. Yoga challenges you to focus on your breath, and it guides you to clear your mind. The belly breathing and mindfulness in yoga help tremendously with stress management.

My favorite yoga pose is the tree, but following the accident it was my most challenging pose. I could not stay balanced at first, but the tree pose slowly helped me re-learn how to balance. The focus required to do this pose helps the body and mind. The tree pose involves standing on one foot and slowly bringing a knee up and out to the side, with the goal of getting the bottom of the raised foot to rest on the inner thigh. It was a slow start for me to return to the pose. I initially started with my foot resting on the floor and worked my way up. It took concentrated practice to get my foot to my inner thigh and stay bal-anced. Yoga brought me peace and continued to build my confidence.

In addition to yoga, another recommendation from Stacia was to start walking outside and exploring nature trails in the area. I started walking within my neighbor-hood. The walking kept me moving and pushed me to be outside. As I moved more, my energy started to increase and my thinking started to become more focused. Walk-ing also allowed me to interact with others in the neigh-borhood. I saw many neighbors and began reconnecting. These walks not only helped my physical health but also built a stronger support network as I was healing.

On this physical healing path, I would often share information about my process with my church friends and I was open to suggestions from others. I listened to any ideas people had for me. One day, my friend Jason told me about his morning bicycle rides on the Fox River Trail. Each day he would ride the trails to exercise his dogs and obtain the peace he found while riding. I was intrigued by his bicycle adventures, which led me to pull my bicycle down from where it was hanging in the garage. I took it to a local bike shop for an evaluation, where they informed me they had not seen that type of bike in years. It was my first Schwinn mountain bike and even had front shocks. The guys at the bicycle shop tuned up the bike and added air to my tires, then I was ready to roll.

I had not been on the bicycle in about ten years. At that time, I lived in the northern Chicago suburbs, and my friends and I frequently rode the forest preserve trails on the weekends. Springtime was my favorite because we would get a bit muddy after the snow melted. I was not familiar with the trails in the western suburbs where I was currently living. Where would I go to bike? What would it feel like? Would I even remember how to bike?

It was a bright sunny morning when I ventured out for the very first time. I told myself to start with small rides to get reacquainted with bicycle riding. The first part was to get used to balancing a bike again. My balance was a bit off following the car accident. I was still healing and had to be cautious with how well I could or could not balance. It took a little bit of time to get used to balancing the bicycle again. It was my first step and a new risk.

I was determined to build a pattern of bicycling for exercise to build my endorphins and get off the medication. I started slow by venturing around only a few blocks in my neighborhood. But I knew I wanted to expand my rides, so I soon began to inquire about good places to ride close to my house. When driving around the area, I started to take note of the signs and parks that had bike paths.

I could always pack up my bicycle on my car, but I was hoping to find a nearby trail. When I felt more confident on my bicycle, I decided to cross one of the highways to pick up a local trail behind the local hospital. I was slightly nervous to cross the highway, but I built up my courage and headed over to explore the trail by the hospital. It was lined with green trees and I was looking forward to where it would take me. I started down the trail feeling full of adventure and then—surprise! The trail flowed right into the back parking lot of the hospital. It was a pretty ride even though it was a short trail. The next challenge was to ride back uphill to get home. I quickly realized I had more work to do on my cardio strength, but I felt accomplished in taking the first ride toward dramatic brain healing.

That first short ride on the wooded trail behind the hospital was a big achievement. It was progress, yet I needed to continue to build upon the first ride. The experience started to bring back some confidence and created a longing for more. Bicycling, in my life, has always been a source of great joy. I remember my very first bicycle with a leopard print banana seat. I loved that bicycle. My bike was not a means for exercise, but for play and enjoyment. Throughout my childhood my bicycle was a main mode of transportation, but it also equated to freedom. Bicycles were a means to adventure and exploration. They were for racing and traveling to connect with friends.

My leopard print banana seat bike brought happiness and freedom. I gained great confidence after learning how to ride, and even more when I learned how to ride with no hands on the handle bars. The bicycle provided courage and a means for problem-solving. I explored deep issues such as what type of noise the bike would make if I ran something through the spokes. I tested playing cards, plastic pieces—and discovered sticks didn't work too well. Riding my bicycle when I was young gave me time to create my own dreams and kept me focused on the present by watching what was ahead on my path.

The short trail ride behind the hospital was the start of something bigger. I wondered what would happen if I followed the trail in the other direction, away from the hospital. I felt excited to be riding again. The first ride after the accident gave me hope; my bicycle created an avenue to reach my goal of releasing all medication.

Hope. Adventure. Direction. These were all a result from the very first bicycle ride after the accident. I was super excited to tell my friend Jason about my adventures. He encouraged me to continue. He was an early morning rider and I decided I was going to be one, too.

I am certain my twenty-year-old mountain bike and I did not have all the necessary accessories to ride, but I made it work. I most definitely did grab my bike helmet for riding—I knew from the accident how easy it is to injure the brain. I thought back to when none of those accessories mattered when I was riding as a carefree kid.

Times had changed.

The day after my first ride, I grabbed my bicycle and rode toward the trail again. I first rode the familiar trail behind the hospital. I packed my courage in my bag that day, and I crossed the road and followed the trail in the other direction. I felt as though I was a child taking baby steps. First, I was getting accustomed to riding a bicycle again. Second, I was building my courage and ability to take risks. Third, I was exploring the world around me in a whole new way. I kept the end in mind, thinking about ways to increase my endorphins, feel better, and get off the medications.

Day by day I grew stronger in my bicycle riding, improving my balance. I started on the small trail rides, but soon found the path led to a busy street before it continued on. I still felt fragile so riding on streets was not my preference. I rode the trail to the busy street and turned around. I had a short and safe trail ride to work with to rebuild my confidence.

Before long, I wondered what was happening further down the trail. My cycling was getting better, I was building balance and endurance. Suddenly, the bike seat didn't hurt my butt anymore. I had to let go of being fearful to step out and explore once again. The accident frightened me and kept me in limited thinking. I needed to follow the advice of The Little Engine That Could, "I think I can. I think I can." I knew that deep down everything would be ok.

Curiosity and my goals pressed me forward toward more adventure. I took the risk and crossed the busy road to the other side of the trail. I had never walked or ridden this trail before, so I did not know what to expect. I was pleasantly surprised to find I was riding along a creek that connected to a beautiful lake. It was an awesome experience. I had no idea there was a lake in the middle of the subdivision. When I take risks and adventures I often find a beautiful surprise, and finding the lake was one of those unexpected blessings.

I ventured to take the trail around the lake, where I discovered hills and arched pathways covered with trees. So my regular biking paths became the trail behind the hospital and the trail that looped around the lake. I later discovered the trail is named Waubonsie Creek Trail. It has hills and twists, and it took some time to build my endurance for riding. The small rides in the neighborhood grew into the rides on the Waubonsie Creek Trail.

I continued to ride the trails and my endorphins increased, greatly helping my sleep patterns. I was able to sleep much less than the twelve hours that had become my norm. I created a new pattern. I went to sleep early and woke up early, often hitting the trails around 6 a.m. The bicycle riding became a wonderful morning ritual. I was growing stronger and feeling more physically fit.

I was grateful to find an activity that was easy to access, allowing me to get moving and improve my health. Each ride was bringing me closer to moving off the medications that dulled my personality and feelings. The endorphins from riding brought new emotions for me, and my personality started to return. Many people's prayers were being answered. God was answering my prayers, too.

My daily bicycle rides were originally for exercise to build endorphins, but they became a much bigger part of my life. Just months before, I could not understand why my friend Jason rode his bicycle religiously every day, several times a day. But I was now experiencing the great joy and peace he felt when riding. I got into the routine where every morning I would wake, roll out of bed, change into my bicycling gear, and hit the trail. There wasn't really any special gear that I used, I just grabbed my two-decades-old bicycle and rode. It may have seemed boring to some people that I took the same trail every day, but the familiarity provided structure, consistency, and a creative way to heal. Armed with my Moab bike and knowledge of a bike trail, I was ready to conquer the world. Well, conquer my world of overcoming a traumatic brain injury. The key to bicycling is to keep moving. This is also true in life.

Wake up, bike. Wake up, bike. This was my journey to navigate the RIDE of change. Risking, innovating, deciding, and enduring—it was the best way to describe my process for change and journey to healing. Biking helped me establish a pattern for a healthy lifestyle adventure. I also added the changes in nutrition to help support my quest for healing. It took time and persistence to prove I could come off the medications and that I was healing physically, emotionally, and mentally. Bicycling became much more than exercise to increase endorphins. It became an adventure, an exploration, a meditation, and a prayer. The adventure in bicycling unfolded with the various changes on the trail. Some changes were due to weather, and others the changing landscape. It always proved to be an excursion as summer bloomed right before my eyes and fall faded into winter.

Bicycling was an exploration with the variations of the many creatures that lived on the trail. I met often with yellow finches and cardinals. I also met with a doe and her fawns. I have met turtles, hawks, beavers, and butterflies. The experience of bicycling was healing through reconnecting me with nature. The exploration kept me learning, growing, and risking. I was experiencing the harmony of life unfold.

My daily cycling became a meditation for me. When I rode my bicycle, I often lost my sense of time. The experience of timelessness calmed my mind and gave me much peace. I spent hours on my bicycle, being fully present and in the moment. I listened to the sounds of nature because I didn't wear headphones when biking. I admired the sunrise and noticed the dew on the grass. I watched and stayed present to the world of nature that I had often ignored or took for granted. I could fully feel the raindrops when riding in the rain. I noticed the branches that lay broken on the trail after a heavy storm. Staying in the present moment while cycling helped me gain perspective on my life. I realized all that is available to me is only in the present moment. When I stayed present, I could see more clearly. It also helped unclutter my mind from fears about my future work, life plans, and healing. The moments on my bicycle were a blessing.

Everyone needs prayer time. Many things unfolded for me while cycling, and prayer was also part of the journey. I thought of people on my rides, and held positive thoughts of them in my heart in prayer. I did a lot of talking to God on the trails. I reflected on my life while riding, and sorted out my problems through prayer. A large part of my prayer life during my bicycle rides was of gratitude and spreading love. As I made new friends my world was getting larger. It was the perfect time to pray for others as I rode. I constantly prayed for my medical team to guide me to healing. I prayed for family, friends, my church, and people I met in the doctor's office. There are always plenty of prayers to be said for others. It helped me to focus outward instead of inward on my problems. I was, and still am, in a constant conversation with God on my bicycle rides. Bicycling was much more than exercise. It was spiritual growth and emotionally healing.

If I woke up crabby and unsettled, it did not take long to get to a state of gratitude on my bicycle rides. I would create a mental list of things to be thankful for as I rode. I even expressed gratitude in the moment for whatever I encountered on the trail. I was appreciative of the flowering trees that left their petals on the trail. I was glad for the puddles I could splash through. I was grateful for the birds that flew over my head, and the hawks that flew next to me were awesome. I started making a point of expressing gratitude on my bike and it brought new perspective to my life. I was part of a much larger universe and divine plan. Bicycling was truly a powerful exercise in mindfulness.

It never occurred to me measure the distance of my cycling until months later. My friend Jason asked several times how long I was riding, but I never knew the time or the distance. I finally ventured out to buy a bike computer. The distance was not my goal—healing was, but I was curious. I discovered from the computer that I was riding six miles per day on my normal trail ride. The miles were adding up but they were not as important as all of the other benefits I received from riding.

I stayed on target and continued cycling to be removed from my medication. Each day I was getting closer and closer. I kept riding. I had the blessing of an accountability partner, Jason, to help check on my progress and keep me motivated. He and I conversed about the status of the trail and the weather impacts on our rides. We also shared the beauty of the sights on our own separate trails.

I continued to build mindfulness techniques on my rides by adding photography. I started carrying my Black-Berry to photograph the beauty on the trails. Through my photos I was able to express my emotions, problem solve, and tell the story of my cycling adventures. Photography is all about how you frame the picture, so it mirrors everyday problem solving. I would seek all the best possible shots when photographing, and in my own personal problem solving. I got the best possible results through reframing the issues to find the most creative answer.

Riding a bicycle may not be the answer to everyone's problems. For me, it provided a bigger solution than I ever would have imagined. It took determination, discipline, and courage to keep riding. At first, the bicycling was meant to restore my physical abilities and improve my brain. It unfolded into an entire holistic journey in wellness. The many dimensions of cycling helped me navigate the ride of change in many aspects of my life. Bicycling, in time, did help me move off all of my medications. It helped restore me back to my old self—actually, a revised version of me. Perhaps, I became Maria 2.0.

The Friends, Family, and Social Support Path

What happened to my sister? What happened to my friend? What happened to my co-worker? These were common questions asked by those close to me during my journey to healing. My family could not understand what was happening, there were so many changes in the person I had become. It was as hard for them as it was for me on this healing journey.

The truth of the matter is, I would have not made it through the recovery process without my family. They played a big role in my rehabilitation. They stayed close to me and monitored my progress with the doctors' appointments and my daily living. My family members listened as I discussed some of the difficult things going on in my life from the physical and emotional changes, as well as the memory loss. There were challenges as they noticed my personality altering throughout the process. I remember one holiday where I was very, very quiet. I completely zoned out at the dinner table, making no effort to join in the conversation. Yet, it was okay. They knew I would recover.

My friends, from many different places in my life, were very supportive of my healing journey. People checked in with me and affirmed I would get better. There were moments when just a simple check-in was very important. It was nice to hear my phone ring and listen to a positive voice on the other end.

I had friends who recommended helpful books as I was gaining strength. One particular book was by Parker Palmer, *The Courage to Teach*. It is about truly following your passion versus following what others think you should do in life. It was a helpful book for me to think about my past career journey, where I was mostly interested in climbing up the ladder in various leadership roles. I read the book and decided that I had more options in my future work beyond climbing the ladder to success. There were many books recommended on the journey. As I started to come out of the haze of the medication, I was also building my ability to read and retain the information.

The first book I read in its entirety when I was feeling better was the book *Head Games* by Christopher Nowinski. He is the former WWE wrestler working with Boston College in studying concussions and athletes. It was insightful to read the personal account of his journey with concussions and chronic encephalopathy. Chris is an advocate for those suffering from brain injuries. I met him and received his book when I attended the Illinois Brain Injury Association Conference where he was a keynote speaker. Chris is the executive director of the Concussion Legacy Foundation, which is making great efforts in regulations for head injuries and professional athletes.

Attending the Illinois Brain Injury Association Conference in October 2010 was an eye-opener in helping me understand the impacts and healing methods of brain injuries. I met many people who suffered from brain injuries and heard about their paths to wellness. It was a great way to connect with others in a similar situation and not feel so alone on my journey. The association also provided many resources, including support groups.

Many colleagues from my various professional associations kept up with me and my recovery. They would often reach out to meet up for a conversation or just talk on the phone. Invites to professional events were extended to me, keeping me in the loop and helping my self-esteem. My colleagues also offered resources to connect me with other people in effort to find new pathways for healing.

I confided a lot about the healing journey with my faith community. I knew they were saying many prayers on my behalf. They also kept watch over me. If I missed a Sunday, a small group session, or a choir rehearsal, someone would immediately reach out to check on me. I was blessed to have their support and kindness.

The many folks in my life helped me rebuild my sense of community and my self-confidence. They were also good at pushing me to move forward. Some might say my community was having intervention conversations with me. The social support I received when dealing with any medical situation helped me remember who I was before the accident happened. People who cared about me would step up and remind me of what I liked to do and how I used to act. They were hoping the real Maria would emerge again. Their affirmations of my progressive healing and restoration helped me feel I could achieve my wellness goals. Who we are is really not only what we think about ourselves but also how we interact with others in our community.

Surprisingly, another branch of my social support was through social media. Before the accident I was an avid person who posted on Facebook about life and the positives. But after the injury I could not find it in myself to post positive statements, so I completely stopped posting. I also stopped posting because I was on disability and did not want to give the wrong impression and impact my benefits. What I did do was scroll through my friends' posts. One woman posted a morning daily affirmation each day. It was always about gratitude, joy, or general happiness. I followed this friend and looked forward to her daily posts. She will never know how much those posts helped me, but I promised myself I would follow her example when I got better, and post many daily positives on Facebook to help others through difficult times. I am glad I was able to follow suit and hopefully help others feel inspired when they may feel down.

My sorority sisters were also very supportive on my journey to healing. They sent me cards, notes, and plenty of emails. They let me know they were there to support me in any way on the healing journey. They kept track of me and sent me ideas for new directions for my career path and maintained a steady stream of emails and calls of support.

I was blessed with several accountability partners once I set my goals to recover completely from the brain injury. I had friends in the Beyond Fitness class who made sure I did my homework and provided coaching. I also had my Fox River Trail cycling friend to discuss each day via email what we had encountered that morning on our individual bike adventure. I had a wonderful therapist to guide me, a career coach to set me on the path back to work, and a tremendous medical team who guided me to full recovery.

I give my family, friends, and community so much credit for sticking with me. When I wasn't feeling great and didn't have much to say, they still contacted me and supported me. Sometimes I would attend things and not really say much, but they were happy to see me and accepted me "as is." I think we all need more people in our lives who love us just as we are. They certainly kept the faith that I would heal and return to the "me" I was before the car accident.

Many people were supportive along my journey. It took an entire team and a multidimensional focus for me to heal. I had family, friends, medical doctors, physical therapists, psychologists, chiropractors, therapists, church friends, holistic healers, sorority sisters, yoga instructors, and many more to help on the journey. Who are your advocates? Who supports you?

The common theme is that everyone around me believed I would heal and move through this difficult time. There were many prayers said on my behalf—a lot of prayers. I didn't find out until later, but many people in my personal circle had placed me on their church prayer lists for healing. People I did not even know were praying for me. I had no idea, until one day I Googled my name during my career search and I found a number of church bulletins with my name on their prayer lists. It was an incredibly humbling experience, and I truly felt the love of God surrounding me on this journey.

We all need social support from people who care about us. In difficult times, we need community to surround us with their love. I felt very loved on my healing journey. People listened to me, cared about me, and prayed for me. They adapted to the new me, full of challenges, and they accepted the healed me when the hardship had passed. My entire support network pulled me through to healing. I am completely blessed.

The Faith Community Path

I have always been a spiritual person, who believes in God, and a church member for most of my life. Because of my holistic wellness perspective, I know that a spiritual dimension needs to be fostered. Therefore, my faith community was a huge contributor in helping me to heal. A faith community, to me, is a place to share time with others around the topic of God. It is comforting to be involved with a group of people who have shared values and beliefs related to how God is working in our individual lives.

I do believe everything happens for reason. The car accident tested my faith in God. I was a member of Faith Lutheran Church in Aurora, and I participated in many small group book and bible studies. My group met on

Tuesday mornings, allowing me enough time to head into work for the day and still teach my night classes. The car accident happened on my way home from a bible study. The beauty of small groups are the prayers, wonderful faith development, and the social support. It was great to have the support of the group as I was working my way into a tenured professor role, and after the car accident I was able to lean on folks in the church to help support me.

After the accident, I heavily relied on my pastor for support. We had many conversational sessions to help me navigate all that was going on during my FMLA status, the medical appointments, and the legalities of being fired from my professorial position. Pastor Rafael helped me see and explore the many spiritual possibilities and answers for the chaos in my life. He listened. He helped me sort out many of my feelings and encouraged me to continue to trust God.

I specifically remember sitting in my pastor's office after I had received the results from the neuroscience testing and the many brain scans. There was a battle in my mind over what I knew and what the results actually said. I was faced with two identities. My old identity was a college professor with a PhD. My new identity, based on the test results, was someone with a very low IQ. It was extremely confusing. I had no idea who I was anymore. Pastor Rafael had good advice for me when he said, "Maria, take one moment at a time." He reminded me to stay in the present moment and take it day by day to see what type of future would unfold in God's plan for my life.

I had always been very career focused, and my greatest fear was to lose my job. Now my greatest fear was happening, and I needed to learn how to cope. It was time for me to explore who I was beyond my career title. As months went by, after being let go from work, I had a lot more time on my hands. My only focus was to get well and show up for all my doctor's appointments. I was no longer teaching night classes so my evenings were free. When he found out I had nothing but time, the music director invited me to join the church choir.

Joining the church choir gave me new focus and meaning in my life. Part of me wondered, *Who am I to praise God in song?* But I joined anyway, and by joining a group at church I was able to feel connected and start rebuilding a community of social support. At the end of choir rehearsals there was a time for prayer requests to be shared. During my most difficult times, I was able to share my prayer needs and receive significant support and numerous prayers.

The church I belonged to had three different service styles, traditional, blended, and contemporary. When I originally joined the church, I only attended the contemporary service and only knew people from that service. But the choir sang at the traditional and blended services, which allowed me to build new friendships with people who attended the other services. It was beautiful to make new friendships after losing so many friends with the loss of my job.

Looking back, I still have no idea how I managed to sing in a choir while I had no personality and was taking all types of anti-depressants. I wasn't my usual joy-filled self, and I just felt awkward. I give a lot of grace to Jason, the music director, for allowing me to sing in the choir when I am most certain I was not singing very well. The thing is, singing in the choir was probably the only thing that kept me alive.

Small group on Tuesdays and choir rehearsal on Wednesdays help me build structure in my life. It was a way for me to connect with people and feel like I was a part of something bigger than my problems. I began taking the stronger medications in November, following the accident. As my personality started to fade away and I sunk into depression, those two groups of people stayed connected to me. They remembered who I was before my personality disappeared, and they encouraged me to get better.

My small group had members of a wide range of ages, from late twenties to late seventies. This allowed me to interact with many different age groups in the church. I was invited to attend the Young at Heart luncheons, the special monthly luncheon for the older members of the congregation. They ate lunch and play games afterward. I soon learned how to play Rummikub and lose gracefully. Playing the games was good for my brain, and the conversations helped my mind find words faster. Most importantly, I made new friends, and having the social support was critical to my healing.

I will always believe that God placed all these people in my life to help me mend. They were all critical in helping me recover and rebuild my identity. One of the biggest wake-up calls I had on the journey came from the prayer shawl ministry. This group of women spend their Thursday nights knitting and praying over the shawls they are creating. The prayer shawls are given to people going through difficult times, such as illness, sadness, or loss from a death in the family. On one Sunday in the spring of 2011, the women of the prayer shawl ministry formed a circle around me and handed me a red prayer shawl. They placed it around me and wrapped me in love. These wonderful ladies told me they were praying for me, and they knew that God would heal me. The gesture surprised me. I knew that only people going through very difficult times received prayer shawls. Their kindness warmed my heart, woke me up, and gave me an awareness of how hurt and ill I was. In my mind, I didn't believe I was sick enough to receive a prayer shawl, but the experience made me rethink my situation. It was God waking me up and letting me know I needed to heal. It was time to take action.

* * *

Knowing more people across all three services at church made me feel more comfortable in joining new things and volunteering more. Contributing gave me a reason to live and made me feel useful. I joined in with helping as an usher and serving communion. In the summer our church offered Vacation Bible School, and I signed on to help with hospitality and to serve as one of the photographers. I was in charge of gathering photos to create a finale slideshow of the entire event. It was a beautiful opportunity for me to utilize my gifts and stay engaged with people. Serving others was breaking me out of the shyness that was created after the car accident.

After a little over a year, and more healing, I was asked to become part of the connections team ministry. It was a team designated to help new members get connected to the church community and to offer opportunities for serving. My participation in this group helped build my self-esteem and confidence. The team had oversight of meeting the new people on a few levels. We met with curious people who wanted to know more about the church at NEXT sessions. These sessions were designed to help people find their own next steps in the church. We also met with people in the new members' class, where we helped them discern their spiritual gifts. We guided them toward getting involved and volunteering in ministries best suited to their gifts.

These opportunities were incredibly helpful for me to stay engaged with people. I could utilize my leadership and organizational skills to rebuild my brain and prepare for my return to the workforce. A year had passed and it was the second fall since the accident when I was asked to take leadership of the connections team ministry. This definitely helped my self-confidence and my ability to lead again. In the beginning there were many challenges, as I was still recovering from so many medications. I had to re-create my thought process in order to carry out the leadership projects. I tended to be more visionary and artistic, having many ideas and visions floating in my head, but I was no longer able to keep this style of working. I organized my mind for each team project in a very logical, project management fashion. I became very linear in my thinking to accomplish tasks and retrain my brain.

This new style of project management in a linear approach created new neurological pathways for learning, leading, and working. People who knew me before the car accident had seen me operate differently with my work. This was a way I navigated change and rebuilt my working style. As I operated this way, I created an effective new way of thinking. Even as I write this book, I can see my linear approach is still my working style. It was a blessing to be able to rebuild my confidence and skills in these serving opportunities.

I had the time, so I was able help on other church

projects to rebuild my skills. I was often called upon to help with photography for various events. I created a catalog of photos of the liturgical season banners for the church with write-ups for each seasonal category. I was able to rebuild my interpersonal skills through serving communion and serving as an usher. Helping others gave me some responsibility and sense of purpose, facilitating my recovery from my lost job identity. My identity was being rebuilt and it was not based upon my career.

Being a part of the Faith Lutheran Church community allowed me many ways to rebuild, restore, and recover. My confidence grew, and I was able to remember more of the things I previously enjoyed volunteering to do. I gained the courage to return to other volunteer roles and activities. After the accident I had to give up many volunteer commitments, such as being a longtime volunteer for my national sorority Alpha Sigma Alpha. I spent many years serving as a speaker and coach at leadership development institutes, district days, and national leadership events. I had placed my involvement with the sorority on hold because of my insecurity to travel with a limited short-term memory. I greatly missed working with the women of Alpha Sigma Alpha and hoped someday to work with the younger generation again.

My world was so much smaller from the car accident, yet I knew I needed to grow and take risks. I had the time to participate in learning activities for self-development, like the Landmark Forum. This program helped me move through the emotions and shame from being fired. It also helped me remember more of my personality qualities and figure out who I wanted to be. I finished the Landmark Forum and decided I wanted to venture back into working with youth. I shared my vision with Pastor Rafael and asked him how I might be able to help him with the youth activities that would be held on Sunday nights starting in the fall. It was then Pastor Rafael created the role of games coordinator. I could finally add a new title to my identity.

The role consisted of finding or creating team building games for the youth at their bi-monthly Christian education events. I was also to serve as hospitality by signing in the youth and welcoming them to the event. With the games, I needed to do all of the organizing, purchasing of supplies, clarifying instructions, and leading the games. This was tough territory as there were about fifty youth involved in this program. It was frightening to pick up the microphone for the first time and be in front of an audience again after over a year of lost confidence.

The role brought me great joy as I started to build relationships with the other adult volunteers and the youth
of the congregation. This gave me another chance to build
my skills for whatever my next career move would be. It
was an opportunity to step into the skill set of training and
teaching, which I had left behind with the car accident.
Time went on and my confidence grew. I was more comfortable with my ability to use my brain logically for work
tasks and appropriately in interpersonal situations. My
brain was healing beautifully.

To summarize, church is not only about worship services on Sunday. It is a community, a family, and a way to
shape and share our gifts and talents. God used the people
at Faith Lutheran and significantly orchestrated a pathway
to my healing. I was very blessed to later serve as an assisting minister at this church, leading prayers, cantoring,
and serving communion. I am no longer part of Faith Lutheran Church, but I am forever grateful for all the ways
the pastor, music director, and many others guided me toward healing. I recently visited the church for a memorial
service and had the chance to reconnect with the people
who helped me on my journey. I was touched to speak

with some of the youth I had encouraged in the games, and I am blessed to continue to keep in touch with many of them who are on their college journeys.

A major component of healing from a brain injury is to be surrounded by a loving and caring community. I highly recommend a faith community as a means to help heal a brain injury, or to work through difficult life issues. God is in the business of fixing broken people. I was tremendously transformed and healed by these experiences, and I am forever grateful. Thanks, God.

The Spiritual Path

A life-changing car accident on the way home from a bible study is what caused me to reconsider my life path. I thought I was on the right track for my life and my career goals. I had a lot of time to think through the entire accident and healing journey. Spirituality is a big part of my personal wellness, and it greatly helped in my recovery.

I had many questions regarding the entire experience. What was God doing in my life? Was He shrinking my life, preparing me for a complete reset? Would all of my worst fears come true? I learned I could give up many of those fears, as they proved to be false. I did question my faith at times, but I also found I was deserving of much good even through my most difficult times. I saw the experience as a complete life makeover and a revamp of my spirit. I can say the experience was very humbling. I thought I was on the right path. However, I learned there was much more for me to do beyond my original career. I learned many lessons on my journey, but one of the most important was to know my career is not my entire identity. I am much more than my career.

On this journey I faced many fears that tested my faith. I learned to trust God further, and to strengthen my faith. I know I can't carry all of my problems alone. I can ask for help and lean on others. The journey proved that I needed lots of help and support, and that I could trust I would be fully provided for and cared for.

Through the journey I was able to reestablish and re-visit old joys in my life, from dancing and singing to photography and overall wellness. It gave me a chance to reset myself to a more balanced lifestyle. I found through reac-tivating my joys, my life had more happiness and meaning. I was pulled toward new purposes like creating the Do What You Love Foundation. The Do What You Love Foundation helps others find elements of life's purpose and meaning to lead happier lives. This would have never happened in my old work role.

I faced depression with grace and courage. I still showed up in life even when it was not perfect. I was more honest and real about my challenges instead of hiding during hard times.

So how did I tap into my spirituality to heal? I leaned on many people and sought a lot of advice. I learned early on that I didn't have many new goals and could not see a path. I waited patiently until one started to emerge. When I did see a path unfolding, I worked on visualizations to guide me. I used visualizations to see myself healed. I drew pictures on paper of my future self, healed and whole. I designed an ideal career story, including the description of the organization and the ideal coworkers. I visualized my health and wellness improving. I stayed focused on bicycling and other activities to rebuild my body, mind, and spirit. I created a holistic visualization that balanced the wellness principles of physical, intellectual, social, spiritual, emotional, occupational, and environmental.

I took advantage of spiritual redevelopment workshops. Specifically, I attended a workshop in 2011 at the Unity Church of Oak Park. The workshop was led by Gregg Levoy, who wrote the book *Callings*. One of the workshop activities included several prompts and exercises to uncover hints to your life calling. The most telling were the callings questions. We answered the questions to see where our passions lived and what we felt our life purpose was. He asked what we were called to do. I met with him after the session to discuss my aspirations to publish a non-fiction book. In June 2016, I hope to deliver a copy of this book to him. Both he and I are speaking at the National Wellness Institute Conference in Minnesota. He is speaking on his new book, *Vital Signs*, and I am speaking on *Navigating the RIDE of Change*.

Another technique I used to move through the tough times from the accident were affirmations. I needed to re-build my confidence and self-esteem. I had all types of affir-mation lists to read. I even kept them posted on my bath-room mirror to read every morning. I had to provide the self-talk to affirm that I knew I would heal, restore, and rebuild my life. I told myself every day that I was love, courage, and contribution to the world. The affirmations helped me be-lieve in my worth. I had to create patterns with affirmations. One tool I used was the Unity Daily Word devotional. I signed up for the subscription to receive special affirming spiritual devotions. Each day I was sent a new affirmation to focus on, along with a list of prayers for the day. It helped tremendously. I partnered with one of my friends and we read the DW each morning and discussed its meaning via email. It was a powerful lesson in positive affirmations and prayer. I still keep this daily practice today.

A big part of moving through the journey was to change my thinking. I had to change my mindset from challenge to opportunity. People get into accidents, have hard times, and make it through. When I shared with a business coach friend the challenge of being fired and the car accident she simply said, "Congratulations. You are now free to move into another adventure in life." The other mindset I needed to look at was in the context of my entire life. A dear friend said, "Maria, this is only a small chapter in your life." That perspective was very helpful. I have had many more years of success and positive experiences versus the two years it took to move through the car accident and necessary healing. Situations can look so big when we are in the middle of a messy life stage. But our lives are much bigger than these challenges.

The other major part of navigating through the brain injury was prayer. I had prayers and difficult conversations with God to express my anger and fears. I prayed for signs of my healing path to appear. I prayed for the right people to come forward and support my healing. I learned how to ask for help, which was probably the greatest spiritual lesson. I had many prayers of gratitude too, for the many miracles that seemed to appear at exactly the right time.

I wrote this section under the title of spirituality, but perhaps it is mostly about the mindset of always expecting good things. I always expect miracles and that good is coming my way. I learned early on, and read many books about how to have a positive mental attitude. Being positive seems to be met with more positivity.

I also learned to be a possibility thinker, to see there is not one right answer, but many. There were many possible paths to healing from the traumatic brain injury. I had to stay open to the possibilities.

One key book I read about going through hard times was *Tough Times Never Last, But Tough People Do!* by Robert Schuller. When reading the book, I was left with the thought that hard times are not always the core of our lives. Hard times happen, and we must move forward through the change. We have opportunity and possibilities. We have to look at our own locus of control and scope of influence. Who really defines and leads our lives? We do!

The traumatic brain injury was a blip on my life path. But it changed the direction of my life. I had to change my mindset to move forward and navigate the ride of change.

The situation transformed my life and who I am. I am blessed for the experience.

The Music Path

Music is a world within itself
With a language we all understand
With an equal opportunity
For all to sing, dance and clap their hands.
"Sir Duke" (a song by Stevie Wonder)

Let the music play. I was five years old when I approached my kindergarten teacher, begging her to let me sing in front of the class. I had just learned "Yankee Doodle Dandy," and wanted to share it with my classmates. That day is etched in my mind as the beginning of my interest and love for music. I did not have the opportunity to study music as I child and felt I had missed something. Fast-forward thirty-eight years later, to when music and singing would save my life.

I had joined Faith Lutheran Church, a church that had a significant musical focus. I attended the contemporary service that had upbeat Christian songs, and was a far stretch from my traditional Catholic upbringing. The music opened my heart and eyes to a new genre of music. Soon I was listening to K-Love radio station to hear the same songs being played at church.

I had tried guitar lessons years before, and had been a djembe drummer since 2000. But music was largely mysterious to me and mainly reserved for car singing and community drum circles. When I was on medical leave, I was exploring many healing methods. The research on healing from drums relates to how a drum replicates the beat of a human heart. The key is to match the rhythm of the drumming to your own heartbeat. I had the time to attend community drum circles, and these circles turned out to be very powerful healers. They brought feelings of joy and playfulness, something I needed to combat all the stress I was experiencing. The drum circles were energizing and peaceful at the same time. After each circle, I felt refreshed and calm. Playing the drums helped me connect in a community, it helped me feel the rhythm of my heart and soul, and it also challenged my brain to connect to the rhythms. I had to keep up with the group and often match the beat of other drummers. Few will argue that playing music is good for the heart, brain, and soul.

I was progressing in my healing from the car accident, using many creative techniques—drumming and dancing, art and photography. I was striving to find the right therapies to help me restore my brain function. My ability to engage in activities increased with the use of Groupon promotions. I could try new dance classes for a low cost and check out painting events for little money. One day, the most intriguing Groupon offer appeared—an offer for voice lessons. I was inspired by the music at my church, and I though this might be a wonderful way to further explore music. Always an avid learner, I had time on my hands and I felt I could take on a new adventure. The scary part of this new adventure was that I did not know how to read music!

I searched the website to find a voice instructor, and I stumbled upon Katarina. She was a professional opera singer who taught voice and piano. I give much credit to people who sing skillfully. There is a lot of technique behind singing well.

Five months had passed since the accident. It was August 2010, and on my very first lesson with Katarina I found myself lying on the floor with a book on my stomach to understand proper breathing for singing. This meant hissing like a snake to control my breath for a longer time, allowing air to come up from my abdomen. Many of the breathing techniques reminded me of yoga breathing. We were trying to create muscle memory for proper breath support in singing. Breathing correctly in singing helps the resonance and the ability to hit the right musical notes. Katarina was a wonderful voice instructor who coached me into singing as an alto.

I had a couple of lessons completed when the music director at church invited me to join the choir, telling me there was always room for more members in the choir. This frightened and excited me at the same time. Jason, the music director said to me, "Look you're not teaching night classes. Why don't you join us? We rehearse on Wednesday evenings." I was nervous because I really only sang in my car and had no formal music training. Jason told me it was okay that I could not read music, he provided CDs with the music we would sing to help us learn the songs.

I was lucky to still be in voice lessons with Katarina as the choir singing journey began. Katarina had identified me as an alto in our lessons, so at the first choir rehearsal of the season in August 2010 I sat in the alto section. It was fairly quick that the altos identified me as a soprano and kicked me out of their section. They moved me to a section where my voice was a better match with other soprano voices. I met my tribe of sopranos and began my church choir adventure.

We had rehearsals every Wednesday night. My fellow sopranos and the music director were patient in helping me learn how to start sight-reading music. I had to learn what mezzo forte and mezzo piano meant in relation to the volume of our voices (moderately loud and moderately soft). I needed to learn what each note meant in terms of timing and counting. This still challenges me today. Perhaps my fear of math kept me from music.

Singing in the church choir provided me another set of friends and community to help me heal. It was neat to meet new people at church who attended different services than the one I had attended. The majority of the choir attended the traditional and blended earlier services. Being a part of the choir gave me a huge growth opportunity to learn music, make new friends, challenge my brain with music, and mainly to praise God through song.

The choir journey had begun. I was given a CD with

the many songs the choir would sing during the first few months of the choir season. I could work with a CD, which gave me the chance to return to singing in my car as I practiced the choir songs. This time my car singing had a much higher purpose. I sang my heart out in the car with the choir CDs.

I was still working with Katarina on my vocal techniques. I had more breathing exercises and several warm-up exercises to work on. She was extremely supportive and taught me many good techniques. I was also strongly mentored by the music director. I was coached by my music director at church to focus on the basics at the beginning. The basics included learning how to breathe correctly in order to sing correctly and how to follow a music director's cue while conducting, which was proving to be difficult because I had to learn what all the gestures meant.

After a few weeks into choir rehearsals, it was time for our first worship singing on kickoff Sunday. Kickoff Sunday is the day all fall church programs start and is considered the beginning of the church year. The choir had rehearsed and I was ready for my first worship singing experience as a member of the church choir. Needless to say, I was nervous. What if I forgot what we were singing?

What if I made a mistake on the notes? My memory was still not functioning well five months after the accident, so I prayed for the best. One of my motivated skills in life is performing, so being in the choir was bringing an element of me back.

The very first worship song I sang in the choir was "All the Earth." I cannot say I remember that song from memory as I had to find the CD recording for verification. I will say that I was completely filled with joy in singing praises to God at the worship service. The experience made my heart overflow with gratitude. I had a permanent smile for a long time. I finally had some sustainable joy in my life following the accident. I looked forward to each Wednesday night for choir rehearsal and to every Sunday morning for singing praise with the church. I finally had new purpose in life!

We received more songs and sang at more worship services. It was an incredibly joy-filled learning experience. I was thoroughly blessed to have a new community and a new learning opportunity to experience music. I was also able to pick up a childhood dream and have it come to fruition. The other beautiful factor was the support I received from the choir community. At the end of each rehearsal, we had a chance to state prayer requests. I had so many people praying for me to recover—they prayed when I had a doctor's appointment and when I was navigating career challenges. The music director kept tabs on me when I did not show up at choir rehearsals. He was a total gift from God.

I was trying so many new things and methods to heal I was not sure what was working. Singing in the choir finally gave me an answer. I was at my neuropsychiatrist appointment and we were discussing all I had been working on to heal. I was sharing with him the great joy of singing in the choir and how I was learning to read music. During the appointment I started singing the lyrics, "One Hope, One Faith, One God," in preparation to sing the following Sunday. The song was running through my mind because I could not stop thinking about singing. Singing was becoming increasingly important to me. I continued singing the lyrics and other parts of the song when Dr. Newsome abruptly stopped me. He stated firmly, "Wait. You cannot do that! You've lost your short-term memory. All the scans show your brain has damage to the frontal lobe where your short-term memory operates. How can this be?"

"I don't know," I said. "I just like the song and the lyrics are coming easier to me. I have to be ready to sing on Sunday!"

On that November 2010 day, in Dr. Newsome's office, we learned my brain was indeed healing. Singing and learning music was mending my brain. We had finally found a solution to help heal my brain. God is so good! Only He would create a way for healing through singing praises and worshipping Him.

Knowing this information gave me strategies to operate in my everyday life. Singing works different parts of the brain. Regular conversation sits in one part of the brain, whereas singing sits in several parts of the brain. My short-term memory was limited, but singing could help. In order to remember things while my memory was impaired, I started to sing them. I was able to go to the mall without fear of forgetting where I had parked my car. I discovered I could sing the location of my car and after shopping I was able to recall where I had parked. I created new tunes from, "A17, A17, I'm parked in A17," to "D11, D11, you'll find me at D11." I created a mental playlist of new tunes to know how to find my car, pick up a prescription, and how to rebuild my life. I had hope!

There are plenty of documented cases of how people with brain injuries were healed by music, or suddenly developed the ability to play music well. People who have strokes often are taught to sing to help recover their speaking ability. Singing and listening to music move across the two hemispheres of the brain, creating more activity throughout the brain. This brain activity creates new neuropathways and helps regenerate the brain. The selection of music also plays a role in stimulating brain activity. Many studies support listening to classical music to enhance brain activity. To heal my brain, I received several musical selections from musicians in my life. Music truly rebuilds and restores the brain.

I can only look at this experience as a true miracle. God used all the right people to help me find this path to healing. God gave me the courage to sing and join the choir as a gift for all the hard times I had been through. The joy was incredible. There were times I would ride my bicycle early in the morning and sing the songs for choir in preparation for the next worship service. Singing + biking = pure joy!

I am still blown away by the doctor saying to me, "You can't do that—but you are. And the singing is healing your brain!" It was simply beautiful and truly a gift from God.

I continued to sing in the choir even through the difficult times of reinventing my life and dealing with the medications. As I continued to sing and learn music, my brain continued to heal. It was exciting and an answered prayer. There were times I had no emotional affect but I kept on singing. People in the choir continued to pray. They were there when I made the choice to come off the medication, change my eating habits, and work with a career coach. They provided ideas and words of encouragement. They urged me to keep singing through the hard times. I was sad to see the end of the choir season that year, but knew I would return in the fall. I had plenty of music to work on to continue my healing. I also had Vacation Bible School to look forward to experience singing and dancing with the kids. I felt like a child coming into learning music, it was an exciting new beginning for me. It was a miraculous way to heal, and I cannot thank enough the music director and choir members for supporting me on this journey to healing and wholeness. I am forever grateful. I am so thankful to God for the healing power of music. Remember when you need to feel joy or clear your head, just sing!

The Arts Path

When I was placed on medical leave to focus on healing from the car accident, I needed to find outlets that would allow me to be productive and creative in the world. I needed to find relaxation, peace, and ways to fill my time because I was no longer working my normal job. Although I have a doctorate in management, leadership, and organizational change, I have a background in art that stems from my undergraduate days when I worked on a degree in photojournalism. Photojournalism is the art of telling stories through photography. During my senior year of college, I had a great opportunity to be a leadership consultant for my national sorority. I had the chance to help other women in sororities nationwide expand their leadership skills, which I found exciting and rewarding. I enjoyed the interaction with other people tremendously. The experience made me realize I wanted to be with people more than

I wanted to be behind the camera lens. I placed my aspiration to become a professional photographer on the back burner, and I allowed my other gifts and talents to emerge.

Throughout my journey I had many doctor and therapy appointments to keep each week all over the Chicago area. Most of the time I felt as though my job was to serve as a professional patient. Yet there was time in between appointments where I had the chance to return to photography. I spent part of the time photo journaling my experiences. I have photos of x-rays, medical gadgets to assess the measurement of my neck mobility, and various brain scans. I engaged in photography during my adversity to creatively express my feelings, not ever knowing where it might lead. I specifically remember one photo of a shattered piece of glass. On that day, I truly felt my life had been shattered into thousands of tiny pieces. The photo was a reflection of what I felt my life had become. Photographing the very hard times on this journey was a powerful healing method that I used to recover what I could of my brain capacity.

I had already been participating in the Capture My Chicago photography contest well before my accident, so being on medical leave afforded me more time to spend on photography. The increased time devoted to taking photos led to an improvement in my skills. Between my therapy and doctors' appointments, my Sony Point and Shoot and the camera on my BlackBerry became my main artistic outlets to find relief. Photography was a way to utilize my brain, express my feelings, and expand my creativity.

One day, by random chance, I went to the Naperville farmers market. I was leaving the market when I noticed an art gallery called the Naperville Fine Arts Center. It houses the art work of the members of the Naperville Art League. It was a magical day for me as I found a new way to grow my photography skills, learn more, and even display my work. I immediately joined the Art League. I had a chance to enter my photos in competitions and gain feedback to build my craft. Competing was a fantastic way for me to keep my creative brain active. I was blessed early on to have one of my photographs selected for the juried members' art show at North Central College. It was a very special day to see my art work on display in an art gallery, and my esteem soared. A reception was held for the show opening and I was thrilled to experience my first artist reception as an artist in the show!

I can remember wondering what an artist wears, trying to figure out the perfect ensemble, even asking friends for their input. The photography offered me a new identity— the identity of an artist. The day of the art show approached and I was elated as I hurried through my medical appointments. Some appointments lasted longer than expected, and I still had to purchase an outfit on the way to the reception. After all of my previous fretting, I ended up picking a simple black dress at the local department store, and cleaning up in their bathroom before heading over. I decided my identity was the non-fussy artist.

That evening at the artist's reception was monumental for my future and my photography. But the day was also balanced with great sorrow. In between doctors' appointments, where I was officially diagnosed with a traumatic brain injury, I also received an email from the VP of human resources notifying me of the termination of my professorial role at a local university. It was an ending and a new beginning all on the same day. Some days we just have to roll with the changes life presents us. We need to learn how to navigate through the ride of change.

* * *

Photography was not only there as a way to build my

creativity and soothe my spirit, it was there to help me with daily life activities. Photography became one of my crutches too. It was a way to help me remember things for everyday living. My TBI was a frontal lobe injury, which greatly damaged my short-term memory. Photography helped. Taking pictures gave me visual reminders and helped me function more easily.

The severity of my short-term memory problem came into greater awareness when I met a friend at a Mercy Me concert at North Central College. I was able to find the concert hall by asking for directions from different people multiple times. However, after the concert I spent more than an hour roaming the streets, trying to figure out where I had parked my car. I was not familiar with the North Central College campus, so I didn't know my way around. It was beyond frustrating, and I was completely embarrassed in front of my friend. After it happened, I realized it was an instance where photography could have helped. From that day forward, I took photographs as a way to remember where I parked my car.

When we have an injury, any injury, we have to seek new ways to adapt for our own survival. As humans we are highly adaptable to an ever-changing world. Change is inevitable and we must learn new tips and strategies constantly. Being flexible is key to not only survival but also happiness. Photography was part of my strategy for survival.

Photography helped me heal, helped me survive, and it also helped provide meaning in my life. By being out of work for so long and being without my normal work social support, I was able to redesign a new community. Walking into the Naperville Fine Arts Center benefited me more than I knew at the time. The ability to focus on my photography was completely cathartic and helped reestablish some of my self-esteem and self-efficacy by being able to participate in art shows. I was able to increase my engagement with the Art League and even participate in entire artist exhibits at local businesses.

As I write this, I realize I was pulled back into something that I loved to help me restore and heal. It was an opportunity for me to reach back into my long-term memory to rebuild my confidence and ability to contribute to others. Perhaps I am making it sound as if it was all happiness on the journey, but it wasn't. There were many times my depression was so severe I did not take any photographs. My life was a black and white photo of nothing—just a shade of gray. I remained active with my photography throughout the entirety of my healing journey, but on many days of dark depression, I did set my camera down. It was a space of nothingness. I had no identity. Nothing inspired me and nothing was interesting. But slowly, as more of the ways I worked to heal took effect, the activities started to provide more help and more reasons to return to my camera.

The return to journaling my life through photographs strengthened me in so many ways. One area of focus leaned toward gratefulness in my life. I found many things that I had rarely taken the time to appreciate before because I was so busy with my career. It was truly the little things that helped me re-examine life and focus on what's important. Beyond photo journaling my daily life, I started to concentrate on what little miracles I did notice and make an effort to show gratitude for them.

There are plenty of ways to work with gratefulness and photography. One way to challenge yourself with photography is to pick a theme for your subject matter. During one part of my healing journey, my theme became water drops. I paid attention to and photographed all the different places I could see water drops. My journey started with the dew drop on some plants when I went bicycling in the morning. The dew became a big focus of my photography as I witnessed a lot of it on the bicycle trail. When the temperature started to drop, the dew frozen on the grass sparkled in the sun. I fondly named it glitter grass. I also focused on water drops after it rained. One of my favorite photographs was of the many daisies in my own backyard sprinkled with raindrops. The raindrops rested softly on the petals, inspiring me to call it gentle rain. Today, I still focus on photographing water droplets.

When we are hurting and need healing, it makes the most sense to return to doing what we love. We often neglect to make time to create art, dance, or sing—but when we do, it almost always brings us joy. All types of art have been a major part of my healing journey and I continue to use these methods for stress release. Creating art and art therapy are proven techniques for stress reduction and personal healing. Photography, in particular, has served me well moving through the healing process and still helps me today.

Photography can be a form of mindfulness. I have to stay completely in the present moment to capture the perfect shot. Photography provides me peace, creativity, and a means for mindfulness. It provides me with perspective on what is happening outside of my own self. I can take walk or a bike ride and by staying aware of my surroundings, I find some great photographs to take. It helps me focus and clear my mind from life's incessant chatter. The author Kurt Vonnegut once stated, "To practice any art, no matter how well or how badly, is a way to make your soul grow. So do it."

Today's Story

It is May 2016, six years after the car accident from which I suffered a traumatic brain injury. I took almost two years to fully move through the career challenges and significantly heal from the brain injury. Am I a different person? Yes. Is my brain healed? Yes. How do I know I am healed from the TBI? I was able to greatly transform my attitudes, ideas, health, and life. I know my personality is much closer to who I was before the injury. I have returned to the workforce in both full-time, and additional part-time work. I am more at peace with myself. Additionally, in 2012, I decided to obtain peace of mind, so I met with a different psychologist who specialized in brain injuries to conduct another round of neuropsychological testing. My test results showed my brain was fully healed and restored. I still consider the main lessons I learned in my traumatic brain injury healing every day. I use the many tools I acquired along the way to continue to keep my brain healthy, reduce stress, and lead a well-balanced life.

I still work with my therapist, at times, to guide my leadership and my ability to be self-led. We have made tons of progress over the many years of working together. I had many career options and decisions to make after working with my career coach. I did venture forward to meet my goal of working in a leadership role for a Fortune 500 organization. While working there I was recruited to an adjunct professor role in a different academic discipline. I balanced working full time and part time in a teaching role. I learned I thoroughly enjoyed teaching at a different college and in a different area, business psychology. But in 2013, I could tell by the conversations where I worked, things were heading for change and I expected a layoff. I was correct. All the people in my job role across the country were laid off. Not too long after, the entire division was dissolved.

I used the tools from my career coach to reposition my resume to academia and started seeking full-time professor roles. The company I had been working for provided me with a new career coach and traditional career support services. I designed a portfolio career blending work and volunteerism. I trained with the Illinois National

Speakers Association's Speaker Academy and launched my own professional speaking and coaching business.

For two years, I was striving for a full-time professor role. In the meantime, I took many new online teaching opportunities to rebuild my online teaching skills. In the fall of 2015, I joined The Chicago School of Professional Psychology as a full-time assistant professor in business psychology and organizational leadership. I created my dream career as a professional speaker and full-time college professor.

Keeping my brain healthy remains a high priority. I continue to use many of the techniques described in this book to stay healthy and build my brain capacity. I work to manage my stress in positive ways. I look to exercise and meditation to give rest and restoration to my brain. For my nutrition, I do not use caffeine and barely consume alcohol. I keep watch of my nutrition and choose foods that make me feel vital and alive. These foods are mainly fruits, vegetables, and lean proteins with limited processed foods. I can feel a difference if I'm not eating brain healthy food. I want my brain to be the very best brain I can have, so I continue to work with nutraceuticals for brain health and maintain a fairly clean eating lifestyle.

I take supplements and utilize the nutrition products from Arbonne International to keep feeding my brain good things. I often attend healthy cooking classes or consult a nutritionist to stay healthy.

I have kept up my engagements with music to keep my brain active. I regularly attend healing meditations, such as crystal singing bowls or gong meditations, as sound therapy. The vibrations help heal not only my brain but also other aspects of my life. I keep a ritual on New Year's Eve to attend a crystal singing bowl meditation to let go of the past and make new intentions for the upcoming year. To keep my heart and brain engaged musically I attend regular drumming circles. The pure joy of playing makes me so happy. I enjoy the brain engagement as I play to repeat the specific rhythm patterns in the drum circle. Often times, the drum circle facilitator will lead these types of activities. It is healing on many levels.

Most significantly, I have continued my musical journey of singing and learning to read music. In 2012 I decided to pursue voice lessons again to continue to challenge my brain and my voice. I continue to praise God through singing in the church choir. I also attend other song-based services in the local area. With singing, I had a great opportunity to serve as an assisting minister, for which I would sing part of the prayers. I continue to praise God through song in the choir. I have had the chance to sing in the Messiah concert at Christmas twice. I have also been a co-producer of a Taizé prayer service hosted at my church. It is a service of songs, chants, prayers, and meditations for peace.

My spirituality and mindfulness continue as I grow my faith through study and serving. I participate in several spiritual and bible studies throughout the year. This keeps me focused on shaping, reforming, and growing my character. I attend retreats to stay centered and experience arts and worship conferences to keep a key focus on my mindset and positive attitude.

I still work with the arts and my photography. I continue to show my photographs in the Naperville Art League, Burning Bush Gallery, and First Friday Aurora events, and competing in photography contests helps sharpen my skills. I launched my own photography sales website on Fine Art America. I still use photography as a journaling tool and for mindfulness, but my skills have advanced with all the new smart phone camera technology and apps. My phone or camera is always ready to take a great photo.

My perspective continues to be focused not solely on my work and career; my identity is much larger than my work. I lead a much more harmonious life now. I understand the joys of being balanced between work and other joy-filled activities. I make time for relationships and friendships.

I still focus on my community and enjoy volunteerism in several organizations. I work to know and support my community locally and globally; my world is expanding in wonderful ways. I feel very blessed.

For physical activity, I practice yoga regularly and stay active with strength training and aerobic activity. I had the chance last year to rejoin belly dancing and perform in a dance workshop showcase. A new and important activity I added is Tai Ji Quan, or Tai chi. This was an activity that was often communicated to me for brain health and healing. The activity pushes the brain to cross the left and right hemispheres by having the bottom part of the body moving in one direction while the top of the body is moving in another direction. It takes a very clear mental focus to participate in Tai chi. It is often challenging to slow down and relax in my fast-paced world. The activity challenges my brain, calms my mind, and forces me to be present in the moment. I highly recommend Tai chi for mindfulness and brain health.

What about my bicycle? I am still riding my bicycle for the many reasons I stated before, such as exercise, endorphin release, mindfulness, and joy. I started cycling in the spring of 2011 and completed over five hundred miles by the end of December 2011. Over the past six years, I have ridden over five thousand miles. It is true that, living in the Chicago area, I ride through all of the seasons and all types of weather. I still love the feeling of freedom and enjoy watching the seasons change. I still have my Schwinn Moab mountain bike but was gifted a used TREK hybrid bicycle by a friend who recycles bicycles. Each morning I wake up and bike! The joys of cycling continue for me, along with the experience of being in harmony with nature. My bicycle and cycling helped me navigate the RIDE of change.

Each day I thank God for the recovery from the accident. I thank God for the many people who played a part in my healing journey. It was all a blessing in disguise. I still believe in miracles—always expect a miracle. Keep on riding!

Navigating the RIDE of Change

Even though we like to keep our routines in life, we have to keep riding through change. What are some changes you have experienced? I have experienced change over the years, some from my choices and some from other's influences.

So what were some of the changes you adapted to in your life? What about the telephone? Cameras? Music?

The first telephone I used was a rotary phone. From there came the touch-tone phone, and the wireless phone was soon to follow. Remember when cell phones were introduced to the market? My first cell phone was the big grey Motorola phone with an antenna and heavy battery. Phones and means of communication have certainly changed, now we can even place video calls from our phones.

Photography has also been in a state of change. When I took a photography class in high school, I used a 35mm film camera and had to develop my own photos in the darkroom. Time passed and the cameras got smaller with the introduction of digital point and shoot cameras. As smart phones came into the market, they came with built-in cameras. Now, I don't head into the darkroom, instead I use my phone apps to edit and revise my photos. I have experienced the changes of photography and I have had to adapt.

How we listen to music has transformed. My music started with an AM/FM radio, eight-track tapes, cassettes, and vinyl records. Music has since moved on to CD's and now to digital, streamed music. Although many people are returning to listening to music on vinyl records, and some people never let go of their eight-tracks!

What do we know about the experience of change? Most people will say they do not like change. Why? Because of the fear of the unknown. It takes time to adapt. We like to have control, but change forces us to let go of the handle bars. We often do not see the positives of change and stubbornly try to refuse it. When we understand change, it is easier to navigate, respond, and adapt.

There are many change models we can learn to understand change. Kurt Lewin simplifies the change process through three stages:

Unfreeze → Move → Refreeze

Let's look at this model in the context of wanting to wake up earlier in the morning to work out as the behavior change. The first step is to unfreeze the current process or situation we want to change. In the unfreeze step, we might start to evaluate what type of workout we want to do. We might want to explore our options of working out at home or at a gym. The second step is to move the current situation. When making a move, we might choose to wake up immediately and not snooze our alarm. We might wake up and test out different workouts at home or the gym. The third step is to refreeze the situation. In this step, we would establish the new routine of waking up early and doing the morning workout we've selected. We would have established a new schedule and kept it going. Morning workouts have then been frozen into our lifestyle.

William Bridges tackles the topic of change in the context of transitions. He explains change transition in three stages: an ending, a neutral zone, and a new beginning. In the first stage of transition—ending—the individual is processing through the ending of a situation. It is a time for dealing with the feelings and changes of the ending. It is adapting to the ending. Maybe a person has just been switched to a different building at work, and they need to cope with the uncertainty of a new routine, environment, and group of coworkers. In the second stage, the neutral zone, the individual is in a time period where the old does not exist, and the future is not yet created. There can be a lack of clarity of what to do next. The person is not clear how things will work in the new building and isn't sure what to do. The final stage is called the new beginning. This is where the individual creates a new way of being, or creates a new experience after the change has occurred. The person establishes a new pattern, and redesigns how he or she will work in the new building.

There are many emotions when moving through change. When an individual first experiences the change, even if it is welcome, there may be feelings of denial. Thoughts of, *this isn't really happening to me*, might surface. The individual may experience resistance to the change, often thinking, *I don't want this change to happen*. As time passes, the individual will start to further explore the new change. The individual might ask what is possible in this change. Finally, the individual will make a commitment to the change. It is a normal process for the emotions related to change.

The work of John Kotter helps us understand the process of change in both an individual and organizational context. He theorizes many steps to create positive change. In the first segment of his model, he creates the conditions for change. He states that there must be an increased urgency for change, time to build coalitions and communicate a vision. This can work with an individual, or when a person is leading change. We can build networks to support our own individual changes and ask for assistance. In the second segment of Kotter's model, the focus is on introducing new practices. This allows for enabling action and looking for quick wins. It is when the individual is finding success in implementing the change. In the third segment, he states a need to maintain and sustain change. This would be the time when a person does not let up and finds ways to make the change stick. The individual would create the right conditions to maintain the change.

Now that we know many of the models for change

and how to work through change, let's look at some other considerations for change. How do we cope with change? One way is to look at how resilient we can be in change. Darryl Conner, in his book, *Managing at the Speed of Change*, lists five characteristics of resiliency:

o   Be Positive - See life as challenging, dynamic, and filled with opportunities.

o   Be Focused - Determine where you are headed and stick to that goal so that barriers do not block your way.

o   Be Flexible - Open yourself to different possibilities when faced with uncertainty.

o   Be Organized - Develop structured approaches to be able to manage the unknown.

o   Be Proactive - Look ahead, actively engage change, and work with it.

Change takes resiliency skills. Keeping the attitude of resiliency helps an individual move through change.

Wellness and a balanced lifestyle help an individual move through change. To stay balanced in life, I have always focused on the wellness model. This model includes the dimensions of physical, intellectual, social, spiritual, environmental, occupational, and emotional. This was the main structure I used in working through my traumatic brain injury. I needed to utilize all types of methods to heal under this model. I still like to assess where I am in these areas of my life on a daily basis. If I feel out of balance, I strive to understand what area might be lacking so I can work on restoration. Balance is hard to achieve. Yet, I feel so much better and productive when I am balanced in these areas. This model has helped me tremendously in my lifestyle and in healing from the car accident.

So what is the RIDE of Change? When I thought back to all that I had endured to heal, I knew there had to be a model for processing all of the changes. I thought about all of the bicycling and the various aspects of the transformation I experienced. I asked myself, *How did I ride through the changes?* The RIDE of Change is a model to take action on change in our everyday lives, personal or professional. We begin with the R for risking. The I is for innovation. The D is for deciding. The E is for enduring. Now let's further define these qualities.

Risking is the ability to take the chance on change, sometimes that just means having courageous conversations. We need to take chances and and start taking action. In the stage of risking, a person needs to look beyond fear.

They need to consider all the possibilities and be willing to take a chance. Change is risky, but so is staying the same. Taking risk is the first step in change.

Innovating is the willingness to explore new ideas and territories, and to think creatively. It is looking at all of the possibilities within the change. People tend to be creatures of habit, but sometimes the old ways do not work anymore. The innovating time is when creativity and possibilities emerge. In my experience, I reached out to many people to gather ideas of how to heal. This helped me in innovating a path to heal. Navigating change needs innovation and new ways of thinking.

Deciding is the ability to select choices and move forward. We can get stuck in change if we are paralyzed by decision-making. Have you ever been in a situation where you missed a great opportunity because you did not make a decision in enough time? Often we can be held back in life when we do not make decisions or we let others make decisions for us. Moving forward in change forces us to take life head-on and make decisions. We need to step forward and decide to change.

Enduring is having the strength to commit to the long road of implementing change. Change takes time and persistence. When we enter change we do not know how long it will take to adjust and adapt to the new change. We cannot change the world in one day, but we can make change one step at a time. We need endurance to stick to and maintain change.

Navigating change on my journey was a call to outrageous courageousness. There are times in our lives when we do not want to make a change, but we are forced into it. We want to resist it, but change will persist. We need to take a courageous stand to risk, innovate, decide, and endure. We need to RIDE through change. Life presents us with many good times and bad times. It's truly a journey. We get flat tires, bruises, we experience change, we lose jobs and money, we can even lose our health. At the end of it all, what matters in life is that we pick up the pieces, embrace the change, grab our bike, and ride on! Remember to keep riding and navigate your RIDE of change.

Personal Action Plan

for

Navigating the RIDE of

Change

The following is a tool to help you navigate change with the step-by-step process described in this book. The model of change is based upon the overarching wellness model.

Physical – physical movement, care for the body; nutrition

Intellectual – taking time to learn new things and grow; reading, study

Social – staying connected to people and interpersonal interactions; community

Spiritual – care of the soul, connections with faith, God, nature, purpose

Emotional – monitoring feelings and relationships with others

Occupational – the work we do, ways to express our talents

Environmental – care for the well-being of the world

Navigating the RIDE of Change

» R: Risking - the ability to take the chance on change; courageous conversations

» I: Innovating - the willingness to explore new ideas and territories; think creatively

» D: Deciding - the ability to select choices and move forward

» E: Enduring - the strength to commit to the long road of implementing change

First, let's understand the change.

Describe a situation of change you are facing at this moment.

Do you like the change? Why or why not?

What challenges do you see in the change?

What are you resisting in the change?

What are you embracing in the change?

What are the possibilities of this change?

Wellness and Change

How will this change impact your level of wellness and well-being?

Will the change impact or enhance your physical well-being? If so, how?

Will the change impact or enhance your intellectual well-being? If so, how?

Will the change impact or enhance your social well-being? If so, how?

Will the change impact or enhance your spiritual well-being? If so, how?

Will the change impact or enhance your emotional well-being? If so, how?

Will the change impact or enhance your occupational well-being? If so, how?

Will the change impact or enhance your environmental well-being? If so, how?

What are the top categories of wellness that could help you navigate change?

Now let's look at creating a plan for Navigating the RIDE of Change in your life.

RISKING

Making change is risky. We need to take risks to grow in life and in change.

What are the possible risks you could take in this change?

How could you implement these risks?

INNOVATING

Innovation takes the initiative to brainstorm all the creative ways to move through change.

What are the many ways you could innovate in this change?

How could you implement these innovations?

DECIDING

Making a decision is often the hardest part in change. Reviewing the options takes time and consideration.

What could potentially hold you back in deciding on moving forward in change?

How can you overcome the hurdle of not making a decision?

ENDURING

Change takes time to plan, implement, and maintain.

Endurance is needed to help the change stick.

What will help you remain consistent in going through change?

What are the outcomes for enduring this change?

Now it is your turn to create your plan to navigate the RIDE of change. Select one possible choice in each category and create your blueprint for navigating the RIDE of change.

Risking:

Starting on this date:_____

I will risk in the _____ wellness area.

I will do this by_____

_____.

Innovating:

Starting on this date:_____

I will innovate in the_____wellness area.

I will do this by_____

_____.

Deciding:

Starting on this date:_____

I will decide in the _____wellness area.

I will do this by_____

_____.

Enduring:

Starting on this date:_____

I will endure in the _____wellness area.

I will do this by _____

_____.

Change takes time. Creating a solid blueprint will help you navigate the RIDE of change.

Keep Riding!

Bibliography

Amen's Brain Health Assessment, accessed June 16, 2016, http://danielamenmd.com/.

Brain Gym International, accessed June 16, 2016, http://www.braingym.org/.

Bridges, W., "Managing Organizational Transitions." *Organizational Dynamics* 15, no. 1 (1986): 24–33.

Conner, Darryl, *Managing at the Speed of Change*, (New York: Random House, 2006).

Kotter, John P., *Leading Change: Why Transformation Efforts Fail*, (Boston: Harvard Business School Press, 2007).

"Laban Movement and Analysis," accessed June 16, 2016, http://www.laban-analyses.org/laban_analysis_re-views/laban_analysis_notation/overview/summary.htm.

Levoy, Gregg, *Callings: Finding and Following an Authentic Life* (New York: Three Rivers Press, 1997).

Maria Malayter's Capture my Chicago page, accessed June 16, 2016, http://www.capturemychicago.com. http://www.capturemychicago.com/users/docmaria

Maria Malayter's Fine Art America page, accessed June 16, 2016, http://fineartamerica.com/profiles/maria-malay-ter.html.

Nowinski, Christopher, *Head Games* (Head Games the Film, 2012).

Palmer, Parker J., *The Courage to Teach* (San Francisco: Jossey-Bass, 2007).

Schein, Edgar H., "Kurt Lewin's Change Theory in the Field and in the Classroom: Notes Toward a Model of Managed Learning," ed. Susan Wheelan, special issue, *Systems Practice,* (March 1995).

Schuller, Robert, *Tough Times Never Last, But Tough People Do!* (Nashville: Thomas Nelson, 1996).

"Six Dimensions," National Wellness Institute, accessed June 1, 2016, https://www.nationalwellness.org/resource/resmgr/docs/sixdimensionsfactsheet.pdf.

Vincenzo Solfrizzi, Francesco Panza, Bruno P. Imbimbo, et al., "Coffee Consumption Habits and the Risk of Mild Cognitive Impairment: The Italian Longitudinal Study on Aging," *Journal of Alzheimer's Disease* 47, no. 4 (2015): 889–899.

Wonder, Stevie, "Sir Duke," by Stevie Wonder, released March 22, 1977, on *Songs in the Key of Life,* Tamla, 7 rpm.

About the Author

With a PhD in leadership and organizational change, Dr. Malayter is known as a Chief Change Agent in navigating the RIDE of change for organizations and individuals. An avid cyclist, her early career work with the US Navy's PREVENT health and wellness training program shaped her continued passion for the wellness and business psychology arenas. Dr. Malayter is a professor of business psychology at The Chicago School of Professional Psychology, founder of the Do What You Love Foundation, and an adjunct MBA faculty member at Concordia University–Portland and Webster University–Great Lakes. Learn more at www.docmaria.com

www.ingramcontent.com/pod-product-compliance
Lightning Source LLC
Chambersburg PA
CBHW060751050426
42449CB00008B/1366